MASTER BUDGETING, INCREASE SAVINGS, UNDERSTAND INVESTING, AND AVOID DEBT

MONEY SKILLS
FOR
TEENS

MADE EASY

WHAT THEY DON'T TEACH YOU IN SCHOOL

NICOLE REAP

MONEY SKILLS FOR TEENS MADE EASY

WHAT THEY DON'T TEACH YOU IN SCHOOL

NICOLE REAP

DEDICATION

To my amazing daughters, Rachel and Madison, whose achievements and character fill me with immense pride: This book is my heartfelt gift to you. It is a compilation of wisdom and strategies that I hope will serve as your compass in navigating the complexities of financial management, both in the present and as you journey forward into the future. My deepest wish is for it to illuminate the path toward financial mastery, empowering you to make informed decisions that lead to prosperity and security. May you always find guidance that inspires confidence and success in your financial endeavors on these pages.

CONTENTS

INTRODUCTION

You're browsing your favorite online shop and boom! There it is—that amazing thing you just had to have, even though you didn't know you needed it until now. Fast forward two days, and the excitement's worn off. Now you're sitting there, wondering why you spent half your allowance on something you might not use much. Sound familiar? We've all been there, snagged by the impulse buy. But imagine if you could flip the script and make your money work for you instead of feeling like it's slipping through your fingers!

WHY YOU NEED HELP WITH MONEY SKILLS

Are you struggling with money matters? You're not alone. This is your guide to mastering financial literacy, navigating digital spending, and tackling big buys. We're here to unlock your money management superpowers. Ready to become a boss at handling your cash? Let's dive in!

Feeling Lost in Money Matters?

Let's be honest: Schools often don't provide all the details on managing your money, leaving many of you feeling lost in financial matters. But here's the bright side: Many others feel the same as you do.

Navigating the Digital Money Maze

Today's world is all about online shopping, digital wallets, and, let's remember, the endless scroll through social media. It's like a whole new game of money management with its rules and challenges. You've got to deal with the temptation to click "buy" on that cool gadget or trendy outfit popping up on your feed.

The Pressure to Keep Up

Are you ever pressured to own the newest sneakers or gadgets to keep up with your friends and social media trends? It's challenging not to overspend when it seems like everyone else has all the cool stuff.

Thinking Ahead About Big Buys

Do thoughts about paying for college, getting your first car, or living alone make your head spin? You're not the only one. Planning for these big-ticket expenses can be super overwhelming when you're just starting to figure out the money thing.

Credit and Debt: The Mystery

Let's tackle a tricky topic: Figuring out credit scores and handling debt. Think of it like a game where the moves you make now can shape your financial health down the road. No need to fret! You can grasp this!

Are you feeling a bit lost or searching for that spark? This book didn't land in your hands by mere coincidence. A friend suggested it or its fantastic cover grabbed your attention. You're on a quest, possibly for inspiration or solutions. So, you're up for the challenge, aren't you?

Think of yourself as a boss handling your cash, knowing exactly where each penny goes. That's what financial literacy is all about! It's like having a secret superpower that helps you make wise money moves, reduces stress, and sets you up for a sweet life. It's your ticket to financial freedom!

WHAT YOU'LL GAIN FROM THIS BOOK

Imagine gaining financial skills early on, skills many wish they had learned earlier. This book is your key to that. Envision this: It's about saving money and steering it towards your natural desires. Are you eyeing that cool gadget or dreaming of a trip with friends? The budgeting techniques you'll learn here will equip you to realize those dreams.

And here's the exciting part: investing. At first, it can seem intimidating, but believe me, it becomes inspiring once you grasp it. This book makes it all easier, explaining the fundamentals simply and understandably. Picture your savings flourishing because you know exactly where to invest them.

Credit cards and debt are not the monsters under the bed anymore. You'll learn to turn them into powerful allies. Think of it like mastering a video game; you're in control once you know the rules and tricks.

And are you earning your own money? We've got you covered. From part-time jobs to kicking off your mini business—maybe selling your artwork or monetizing your gaming skills—you'll learn how to make money doing what you love.

This book is about simple financial talk. It's about honest, down-to-earth advice that fits into your everyday life. By the end, you'll handle your cash like a pro, ready to confidently take on your financial future. It's more than just a book; it's your ticket to becoming financially savvy, a superpower you'll thank yourself for forever.

EXPECTED RESULTS FROM READING THIS BOOK

Have you ever thought that handling money should be more straightforward? Good news! There's a method to becoming savvy with your finances, specially designed for you, today's teens. This book is far from the typical boring finance guide. It's like having an excellent mentor who speaks your language and understands your interests.

Let's dive into making your money do the heavy lifting for you. Ready to level up your financial skills and become a cash-savvy whiz? Forget the boring old idea of budgeting. Are we talking about planning your cash flow for epic stuff like a top-notch gaming setup or a fantastic road trip with your friends and saving and investing? They're not just for grown-ups. I'm here to guide you through easy-to-follow, teen-friendly tips using real-life examples that you'll get. You're about to watch your bank account grow in ways you never imagined!

Let's go digital! You're already savvy with everything online, so why not become a pro at digital finance? This guide will teach you how to handle online banking and investment apps expertly and make wise decisions in digital finance.

Building healthy financial habits is like leveling up in a game. You'll learn to spend wisely, save regularly, and invest thoughtfully. These skills are your power-ups for financial success.

You'll uncover the ins and outs of credit scores, wise credit card usage, and the significance of responsible debt management. Think of it as grasping the playbook for a fresh game, enabling you to excel in your financial journey.

Have you ever considered the idea of creating your income? This guide isn't just about saving money; it's all about spicing up your cash flow with remarkable entrepreneurial strategies. It's time to let your creativity shine and explore fresh ways to supercharge your wallet!

What can you gain from this? Confidence! You'll equip yourself to handle financial choices, from daily ones to significant plans. Bid farewell to money-related stress and welcome preparedness for adult financial duties. This knowledge empowers you to save and establish a base for a secure and self-reliant financial future.

You'll become more conscious of how your choices affect your finances and be ready to reach your economic aspirations, whether substantial or minor. Prepare to conquer the world, advancing your financial journey one wise step at a time!

WHY IT WAS HARD TO BE FINANCIALLY SAVVY BEFORE YOU READ THIS BOOK

Guess what? Before the fantastic tips and tricks you'll dive into, learning about money skills was like trying to solve a Rubik's cube blindfolded. Sounds harsh, right? Well, it was!

Back then, teens like you were left to figure out the money maze independently. Think about it: No snazzy apps, no online games to make learning fun, just plain old trial and error. And errors? There were plenty! Imagine saving up for that dream video game or skateboard only to realize you've spent too much on snacks and movies. Bummer!

Get ready for a game-changer. This book is your golden ticket to mastering money! Imagine unlocking the secrets to transforming your allowance, birthday bucks, or earnings from your part-time gig into an ever-expanding pile of cash. This isn't just a book; it's your guide to a treasure trove of financial know-how. Let's dive into making your money multiply!

The old days of money management were as dull as staring at a wall waiting for paint to dry. Seriously, words like "budgeting" and "savings" could almost put you to sleep. But those days are gone! This book is here to turn you into a master of money and believe me, it's a lot more awesome than you think.

Let's start with a real kicker: Did you know that before all these new methods, teens hardly had any clue about credit scores or how debt works? Yikes! Imagine if walking into adulthood was like stepping into a maze blindfolded. Now, we've got your back with the nitty-gritty on using that plastic card wisely and staying clear of the debt trap.

Have you ever had your eye on something extraordinary only to check your wallet and find it practically whispering, "Nope"? We're about to turn that around.

You're not just going to learn about saving pennies in a piggy bank. We're talking about grown-up stuff like investing—yes, even teens can do it! Picture this: you, yes YOU, making money from your money. Sounds pretty epic, right?

Ever feel like all that money chatter sounds like a foreign language? Well, say goodbye to the confusion! We'll break down all those fancy financial terms into easy-to-understand language. Like an expert, get ready to chat about assets, debts, and how interest rates work. You'll be talking money lingo like it's your first language!

Leave those yawn-inducing finance classes behind—this is far from dull! Brace yourself for an exhilarating voyage into the world of money. It's akin to uncovering an undiscovered superpower you didn't realize you possessed. You'll become a pro at making smart financial choices, aiming high (think fantastic cars and epic adventures with pals), and watching your savings thrive.

So, if you're ready to take control of your cash, make informed decisions, and set yourself up for a future where money worries are a thing of the past, this is the book for you. Say goodbye to confusion and hello to being the boss of your finances.

Get ready because, with this book, you're not just saving money but setting the stage for a lifetime of financial wins.

CHAPTER ONE

THE FOUNDATIONS OF FINANCIAL SAVVY

P icture this: You've been stashing away cash for the newest gaming console, and guess what? When you're ready to snag it, you find out you've also got enough dough for that concert ticket you thought was out of reach. This success is due to your pro-level budgeting skills, not just luck!

BUDGETING BASICS

Let's chat about budgeting—it's not just for adults! Do you know how you plan out your day? Budgeting is like that but for your money. It's super crucial, especially for you.

First off, budgeting is all about setting goals and making choices. Want that new game or gadget? A budget can help you save up without going broke. Grasping the difference between needs (such as food and clothes) and wants (like the newest phone) is crucial. Master this early, and you're on your way to success. Your future self will be grateful!

Stats show that teens today understand the importance of budgeting. Ninety-three percent of you believe financial knowledge is critical to reaching your dreams. But there's a catch: While you're smart about money, many still score below 70% on financial literacy tests (*Survey Finds*, 2022). This means there's a gap between what you know and what you need to know.

Now, how are you managing money? Surveys reveal that about 54% of teens feel unprepared for their financial futures and 62% use mobile apps for money management (*Teenage Money*, n.d.). That's a good start! Budgeting apps or prepaid cards can make learning about money more accessible and hands-on.

Here's the cool part: When you start budgeting, you learn to value money more. Whether saving for a concert ticket or buying your clothes, handling your cash gives you a sense of achievement. Plus, you start understanding big goals like purchasing a car or saving for college.

Simple Steps to Create a Basic Budget

It's fantastic that you're thinking about budgeting and managing your money at a young age. Let's dive into some straightforward steps to help you create a basic budget and grow your money wisely:

- **Know your income:** Start by determining how much money you bring in. This income might come from sources such as allowance or part-time jobs. Remember, knowing your income helps you make intelligent decisions about spending and saving.
- **Create budget categories:** Break down your expenses into categories like savings (for college, a car, or even retirement), necessary expenses (like gas or phone bills),

and other expenses (like gym memberships or eating out).

- **Pick a budgeting strategy**: You've got a few fantastic options here:

  o **"Pay yourself first" strategy**: Set aside some of your income for savings before you begin spending.
  o **Zero-based budgeting**: Allocate every dollar you earn to specific expenses, leaving no dollar unassigned.
  o **50/30/20 rule**: Allocate 50% of your funds for necessities, dedicate 30% to your desires, and set aside 20% for savings.

- **Save first, spend later**: Try to save a portion of your income before you begin spending. This habit guarantees that you're consistently increasing your savings.
- **Set goals**: Consider your financial goals and what you aim to accomplish with your money. It could be saving for college, a new gadget, or even starting a small business.
- **Track your habits**: Stay vigilant about tracking your money's whereabouts. This can help you understand your spending patterns and adjust as needed.
- **Adjust your budget**: Don't be afraid to tweak your budget if it doesn't fit your needs. Flexibility is critical to successful budgeting.
- **Learn from your mistakes**: Making mistakes is alright; however, it's crucial to learn from them and adjust your budget.
- **Earn more with a side hustle**: If you're looking for more budget flexibility, consider earning extra money with a side hustle like dog walking, tutoring, or selling baked goods.
- **Be a spending minimalist**: Embrace a minimalist approach to spending. This means valuing quality over

quantity and being mindful of your purchases.

- **Don't give in to peer pressure:** Stick to your budget even if your friends are spending more. It's perfectly fine to decline costly outings and propose more affordable activities.
- **Seek out help:** If you have any uncertainties, seek guidance from your parents, teachers, or financial mentors.
- **Have fun:** Remember, budgeting isn't just about restrictions; it's about making intelligent choices that allow you to enjoy your money too.
- **Follow money-minded influencers:** Check out social media for financial advice tailored for young people. Influencers like Humphrey Yang (@humphreytalks) and Tori Dunlap (@Herfirst100k) offer great tips on saving, investing, and managing money.

By taking these steps early on, you're laying the foundation for a financially savvy future for yourself. Remember, it's about balance —saving for tomorrow while enjoying today.

How to Track Income and Expenses

Effectively managing your money is crucial for financial independence, especially for teens. Here's how you can do it:

- **Understand your current spending:** Start by gathering data on your spending habits. Collect receipts and track every dollar spent for at least a week, preferably a month. This will help you see precisely how you're spending your money. Tools like bullet journals, spreadsheets, or banking apps can be helpful. For instance, 62% of teens use mobile apps for money management (*Teenage Money*, n.d.).

- **Income sources:** As a teenager, your income might come from allowances, part-time jobs, or gifts. In 2022, teens were likely to spend around $2,367 yearly, mostly from their parents. Typical jobs for teens include cashier, waiter/waitress, and retail salesperson, with an average hourly wage of around $10.03 (*Teenage Money*, n.d.).
- **Expense categories:** Be aware of your typical expenses. In 2020, the average teen spent $2,150 across categories like food, clothing, and entertainment (*Money Management*, n.d.). It's crucial to grasp your spending habits and patterns to create a budget that suits you best.
- **Set financial goals:** Define your short-term and long-term financial objectives. This could be saving for college, a car, or simply building a savings cushion. Remember, even regularly saving a small amount can grow over time.
- **Use budgeting tools:** Leverage tools like Bank of America's Spending & Budgeting Tool or other online resources to help you track spending and stick to a budget. These tools can assist in spotting trends and managing your finances more effectively.
- **Financial literacy:** Educate yourself about financial basics. Surprisingly, only 24% of millennials in the US understand basic economic principles (Radic, 2023). Use online resources, financial literacy apps, or educational games to boost your knowledge.
- **Monitor and adjust:** Stay vigilant with your budget and make any needed adjustments. Your spending and income can shift over time, so ensure your budget remains adaptable to these fluctuations.

Successful money management hinges on being aware and disciplined. When you know the sources and destinations of your money, you can make informed choices and establish a sturdy financial groundwork for your future.

THE ART OF SAVING

Saving money is vital, even on a small income, and there are several effective methods for doing so, especially for teenagers. Here's a brief guide to kickstart your journey:

- **Open a savings account:** This is your first step. Choose a bank that suits your goals, whether you're saving for a new laptop or your first car.
- **Use your savings account:** Just opening an account isn't enough. Regularly deposit a portion of your earnings, gifts, or allowance into it.
- **Start earning to start saving:** You can earn money through summer jobs, internships, or even chores at home. This lesson helps you understand the significance of money and the necessity of saving it.
- **Set a goal for yourself:** Whether for college, a vacation, or a big purchase like a car, setting goals helps you stay focused and motivated.
- **Make a budget:** Identify your needs and wants. Allocate your income using the 50-20-30 rule: 50% for needs, 20% for wants, and 30% for savings (*7 Important*, 2023).
- **Stick to your budget:** Consistently review your budget and make essential changes. This helps you stay on track and avoids overspending.
- **Use an app if needed:** Budgeting and money management apps can help you track your expenses and savings goals more efficiently.
- **Save on expenses:** Be a savvy shopper. Look for discounts, use coupons, and consider generic brands over name

brands to save money.
- **Plan and stay motivated:** Set short and long-term goals. Planning for future expenses like college or a car will help you stay motivated to save.

It's important to note that the average American teenager saves about $548 to $720 annually (*Teen Saving Statistics,* n.d.). This saving behavior is crucial as it impacts lifetime earnings, financial stability, and even mental health. Early saving can allow you to make the most of compound interest, substantially boosting your savings as time goes by.

Tips on Setting Saving Goals

Setting savings goals as a teenager is empowering and essential for your future financial success. Here are some tips tailored for you:

- **Identify your financial priorities:** Your goals range from saving for a new phone to funding your college education. Remember, what matters to you is what's important.
- **Earn your own money:** Whether it's a part-time job or doing chores for neighbors, earning gives you a sense of independence and responsibility towards money.
- **Learn to budget:** Track your income and expenses. Apps or simple spreadsheets can be great tools here. Comprehend your spending and pinpoint savings opportunities by tracking your money's destinations.
- **Pick the right financial tools:** Research and use tools that fit your requirements. This could be a savings account with a reasonable interest rate or an app that helps you track expenses.
- **Start long-term savings:** Think about the future. It's never too early to save for long-term goals like college or a car.

- **Stay motivated:** Only about 9% of people accomplish their New Year's resolutions (C., n.d.). To stay motivated, set achievable goals and keep tabs on your progress.
- **Put spending into perspective:** Ask yourself, "Do I need this or do I want this?" This simple question can help you avoid unnecessary expenses.
- **Map out additional costs:** Consider all costs associated with your purchases. For example, consider insurance and maintenance expenses when saving up for a car.
- **Encourage independence:** Being financially independent is liberating. The more you manage your finances, the better you'll get at it.

Remember, setting and achieving savings goals isn't just about the money—it's about building habits that will serve you well throughout life.

UNDERSTANDING TAXES

Let's break down what taxes are all about and why they're essential for you to understand, even as a teenager.

First, taxes are like a membership fee for living in a country. This cash goes to the government for cool stuff like keeping our schools running, fixing roads, and ensuring we have fire departments and parks. Taxes even fund programs like Social Security and Medicare. Without taxes, governments couldn't provide these essential services.

Now, how do taxes work? When you start working, a portion of your salary goes to taxes. In the United States, the Internal Revenue Service (IRS) is responsible for gathering federal income taxes, and your earnings determine the amount deducted. The amount they deduct relies on your income. For instance, in 2023, if you're single and earn up to $11,000, you're taxed at 10%. Earn more, and the percentage increases, hitting different brackets as you earn more (Durante, 2022).

If you're a teen working a part-time job, filing a "Simple Tax Return" is probably your best bet. This is pretty straightforward and requires your W-2 form (which shows your income and taxes paid), legal name, birth date, and Social Security number (Anglin, 2023).

But here's a fantastic part: not all teens need to file taxes. If your job has withheld taxes or you're eligible for a refund, such as the American Opportunity Credit, it's wise to file your taxes. You must file if your unearned income (like from investments) is over $1,100 or your earned income is more than $12,550 (*Tax Filing Requirements*, 2023).

Filing your taxes is a smart move. It might help you qualify for college scholarships or financial aid through FAFSA that you wouldn't get otherwise. Additionally, if you've paid too much tax from your paychecks, you might earn money back from the government!

Remember, there are other types of taxes, like sales taxes (on stuff you buy) and property taxes (if you own property). But as a teen, you mainly deal with income taxes from your job.

Navigating taxes can be tricky, especially when starting with a part-time job or maybe a summer gig. Let's break it down with some examples so it's easier to understand.

At 17, you may have secured a part-time job at a neighborhood café. You've earned about $10,000 this year. Great job! Now, it's time to talk taxes. For the tax year 2023, if you're under 19 or a student under 24, you'll need to file a tax return if your earned income is more than $13,850 (Allcot, 2023). Generally, you wouldn't owe taxes if your earnings are below a certain amount. However, filing a return could still be beneficial to reclaim any income tax withheld from your paychecks.

Let's say you also did some tutoring on the side and made $2,300, plus you sold some cool Harry Styles merch for $300. That counts as earned income. And, if you made $500 from investing in stocks like DraftKings, that's unearned income. Even if these amounts are below certain thresholds, you still need to file a tax return because your total gross income is more than $2,700, a combination of your earned income plus $400 (Kosoff, 2023).

Also, reporting these earnings is essential if you received tips at your café job. You need to file a record of your tips with the IRS to pay Social Security and Medicare taxes on this income. If you made more than $400 in tips, you should include this in your tax returns (Allcot, 2023).

Remember, the numbers I've mentioned are specific to the tax year 2023 and could change. It's always wise to consult the latest tax guidelines or chat with a tax professional when uncertain. Filing taxes might seem daunting initially, but it's a valuable skill that'll benefit you throughout your life. Plus, who doesn't like getting a tax refund, right? Continue your outstanding efforts, and remember, if you need assistance, don't hesitate to seek it.

STORIES OF TEENS WHO BECAME SUCCESSFUL WITH BUDGETING AND SAVING

Story 1: The Dream Camera

Let me tell you about Jamie, a 16-year-old passionate about photography. Like you, Jamie had big dreams and an even more significant challenge: saving enough money for a professional camera. Does this sound familiar? Well, here's how Jamie made it happen.

Jamie set aside some of their weekly allowance and money from odd jobs. Yeah, it meant skipping those tempting weekend outings with friends sometimes. But guess what? Jamie had a clear goal in sight. They even started a small online business selling handmade crafts. Smart, right?

You won't believe this, but Jamie had enough for that camera in just eight months. Imagine the pride and excitement! The best part? With each photo Jamie captured, she recalled the dedication and effort it had taken to reach that point. So, think about what you're saving for. Like Jamie, you can make it happen with a bit of patience and a lot of determination.

Story 2: Dad Turned Dimes Into Dreams

Alex, a vibrant teenager with dreams more significant than his allowance, often found himself in a pickle. His goal? A shiny new bike to join his friends on weekend trails. But alas, his piggy bank echoed with emptiness.

Enter Jim, Alex's dad, a wizard with numbers and a heart as big as his budget sheets. One sunny afternoon, Jim sat down with Alex, their kitchen table transforming into a mission control center for Operation: Bike Fund.

"Alex, let's make your dream a reality!" Jim exclaimed, his eyes twinkling with excitement. He pulled out a colorful chart, making numbers look like a fun game rather than a tedious chore.

Together, they outlined Alex's weekly allowance and expenses, from those sneaky snack purchases to the essential movie outings. Jim's approach was simple yet effective: "Save a little, enjoy a little."

Each week, they had their "Finance Fridays," a time for laughter and learning about money matters. Alex discovered the joy of seeing his savings grow, penny by penny. Jim's unwavering support and clever tips made budgeting feel like an adventure rather than a task.

A few months later, Alex's brand-new bike gleamed in the sunlight. The journey taught him more than saving money; it brought him closer to his dad, turning financial lessons into life-long memories.

And so, Alex pedaled into the sunset, his heart full, his wallet wiser, and his dreams just a bike ride away.

How to Avoid Common Mistakes About Money

Navigating money matters as a teen can be tricky, but I have some tips to help you dodge common financial blunders:

- **Budgeting is key:** Sailing without a map is similar to not having a budget—you must understand where your money is flowing. Craft a straightforward budget to monitor your spending and saving habits.
- **Save for the future:** Spending all your cash now is tempting, but saving for future goals or emergencies is crucial. Even a little bit saved regularly can add up.
- **Wants vs. needs:** That latest gadget or fashion item might be cool, but is it necessary? Spend wisely by differentiating between what you like and what you need.
- **Credit cards: Handle with care:** Credit cards are not free money. Use them responsibly to avoid debt and build a good credit history.

- **Smart car choices:** Dream cars are fantastic, but expensive loans? Not so much. Consider more budget-friendly options like a second-hand car or public transport.
- **College costs:** Education is essential, but so is avoiding massive debt. Search for scholarships and grants while working part-time to reduce your financial load.
- **Live within your means:** To prevent debt, ensure you don't spend more than you earn. Keep a vigilant watch on your expenses and adhere to your budget.
- **Invest wisely:** Tempted by risky investments like crypto? Remember, high risk can mean high losses. Begin with safer investments and gain knowledge as you progress.
- **Be careful with money and relationships:** Lending money to friends or sharing bank accounts can get complicated. Think twice before mixing money with friendships or romantic relationships.
- **Independence is key:** Relying on parents to bail you out isn't a long-term plan. Learn how to handle your finances and become self-reliant.

Remember, it's about making smart choices now for a financially secure future.

PERSONAL BUDGET PLANNER

I've got some excellent news for you. Use our fantastic printable budget planner templates to manage your monthly income and expenses actively. Let's dive into what I found:

- Money Prodigy's Teen Budget Worksheets: These worksheets are perfect for tracking your income from allowances, part-time jobs, or even birthday money. You'll also get to record your expenses, like your cell phone plan or those irresistible vending machine snacks. The best part? There's a section for savings, encouraging you to "bank" your leftover cash at the end of each budget cycle. Plus, there's a handy money calendar for planning.

URL: https://www.moneyprodigy.com/teen-budget-worksheets/

- Printables and Inspirations' 2024 Budget Planner: This one's a gem! It comes with 20 pages of budget planner worksheets, including an annual bills tracker and a monthly budget page. You can monitor your savings and keep track of your expenses categorized. It's a great tool to understand your spending habits and plan for the future.

URL: https://www.printablesandinspirations.com/budget-plan ner-worksheets-printable/

- Printable Formats' Budget Templates for Teenagers: These templates, designed for weekly, bi-weekly, monthly, and yearly budgeting, are super user-friendly and offer a wide range of options. These tools can track your income and expenses effectively, providing you with a clear understanding of your financial well-being. The templates are easy to use and come with cool features like graphical presentations of your budget.

URL: https://www.printableformats.com/budget-templates-for-teenagers/

Remember, using a budget planner isn't just about tracking where your money goes. It's about making intelligent choices and setting yourself up for a financially secure future.

KEY TAKEAWAYS

- Budgeting is essential for teens, helping differentiate needs and wants, and is crucial for achieving financial goals.
- Using a budget planner helps teens appreciate the value of money and achieve savings goals like concert tickets or new clothes.
- Effective budgeting involves knowing your income, categorizing expenses, choosing a budgeting strategy, and setting financial goals.
- Setting realistic saving goals and using appropriate financial tools are critical for teen financial success.
- Understanding taxes, like income and sales taxes, is vital for teens, especially when working part-time.
- Avoiding common financial mistakes includes smart budgeting, saving for the future, understanding wants vs. needs, and using credit cards wisely.

You've mastered budgeting and saving—excellent work! Ready for the next level? Let's explore how you can use credit smartly and avoid falling into debt traps. We'll dive right into it and make sure you're on the right track!

CHAPTER TWO

CREDIT AND DEBT—MANAGING FINANCES WISELY

I magine this: You've just got your first credit card. It feels like you've unlocked a new level in a video game where you can buy all the cool stuff you've always wanted. But here's a key point: Using a credit card isn't the same as having free money. Instead, it's borrowing money you need to repay, with interest added.

Think of it like this: You're at a candy store and you've got this card that lets you take as much candy as you want. But later, you have to pay for all the candy you took and a bit extra for every day you kept it. If careless, you could owe much more candy than you initially took!

Before you get excited about having a credit card, let's unravel the truth about credit cards and debt and why understanding these can be your secret weapon for financial success.

UNDERSTANDING CREDIT

Let's discuss credit, a super important topic for your financial future. Think of credit as a trust exercise with money. Using credit means you borrow money now and promise to repay it later. It's like taking out a loan to get something you need or want when you don't have the cash.

Credit isn't just about credit cards—there are loans and mortgages, too. You can use a loan to buy a car or fund your college education, and a mortgage helps you purchase a house. Each type of credit has its own rules and uses, but they all share one thing: You must repay what you borrow.

Now, let's explore the realm of credit scores. Suppose your credit score is your school report card. But instead of your performance in your studies, a credit score reflects how well you handle borrowed money. This three-digit number is a tool that lenders, landlords, and occasionally employers use to assess your financial management abilities. The higher your score, the more favorable impression you create. A strong score opens doors to obtaining loans with lower interest rates, which ultimately saves you money in the long term. Additionally, it paves the way for renting a fantastic place, acquiring an outstanding credit card, or landing an excellent job.

Building a solid credit history is super important, and you can kickstart it with some simple steps. First, open a savings account or ask your parents if you can be an authorized user on one of their credit cards. These actions demonstrate that you're savvy with your finances. Another choice to think about is a secured credit card. Here's the deal: You put down a deposit, which becomes your credit limit. It's a great way to learn how to handle credit wisely while reducing the chances of getting into debt.

Prompt bill payment is crucial because if you're late, it can damage your credit score. Also, use less than 30% of your available credit (Plaut, 2023). It shows you're not just maxing out your cards every chance you get.

Finally, stay on top of your credit report and score. You can quickly check your score for free using some websites or apps. Always ensure that everything in your report is accurate. If something seems off, take steps to correct it right away.

Remember, using credit wisely can open many doors for you in the future. It's all about being responsible and making wise choices. Good luck on your journey to building great credit!

Types of Credit for Teens

Let's explore the various credit types you as a teen might consider:

- **Credit cards:** To build your credit history effectively, opt for a credit card that doesn't charge an annual fee, provides cashback rewards, and allows you to apply even without a credit score.
- **Loans from banks:** If you have a bank account, consider a loan for big purchases like a car or education. Remember that while banks provide different types of loans, they might sell your loan to another party without informing you.
- **Credit unions:** Credit unions, like banks, often offer lower interest rates because they operate as nonprofits. However, membership is a must to use their services.
- **Peer-to-peer lending:** Instead of borrowing from a bank or credit union, you get a loan directly from another person. This approach offers a more personal touch to lending money.

- **401k or retirement account loans:** You can borrow against your retirement savings, which is often tax-free. However, remember that the institution, not you, sets the loan terms.

Every choice has advantages and drawbacks, so the key is to find what's best for you. Building credit is similar to leveling up in a game—you need patience and intelligent strategies!

THE DOS AND DON'TS OF CREDIT CARDS

Using a credit card wisely is critical to managing your finances effectively, especially as a teenager stepping into the world of credit. Here are some practical tips:

- **Set up autopay:** You always pay on time by setting up autopay. Remember, missing a payment can damage your credit score and incur extra charges. You can autopay either the minimum amount due or the total balance.
- **Use your credit card like a debit card:** Only spend what you can afford to pay off in full each month. This habit helps you avoid accumulating debt.
- **Only carry a balance during intro APR periods:** If your card offers a lower APR during an introductory period, carrying a balance for a while might be acceptable. But remember, paying it off before this period ends is crucial to dodge those high interest rates.
- **Keep credit utilization below 30%:** The credit utilization ratio gauges the amount of credit you use from your total credit limit. To benefit your credit score, keep this ratio under 30% (Plaut, 2023).

- **Know when to upgrade:** If you've been responsible with your current card, you might be eligible for cards with better terms or rewards.
- **Define your rewards strategy:** Use rewards wisely if your card offers rewards. Opt for rewards that match your spending habits, like cashback, on everyday purchases, but be careful not to overspend to earn rewards.
- **Reconsider canceling your card:** Keep your older accounts open to benefit from a more extended credit history. Use these older cards from time to time to maintain their activity.
- **Understand interest rates and fees:** Know your card's fees and interest rates. Avoid actions that incur high fees, like cash advances or exceeding your limit.
- **Monitor your credit Score:** Make it a routine to monitor your credit score frequently. This way, you can track how your financial choices impact it. And remember, always review your credit report to spot any mistakes.
- **Stick to a budget:** Use your credit card only for items you've already planned to purchase and can comfortably afford within your budget. This method will assist you in effectively handling your debt and avoiding overspending.
- **Debt repayment strategy:** If you have multiple card debts, consider strategies like the snowball or avalanche methods to pay them off efficiently.

Keep in mind that credit cards are like tools—use them smartly. You can achieve more financial freedom by building up your credit history and gaining more financial freedom. Always spend what you can afford and wisely choose when using your credit card.

Common Credit Card Traps and How to Avoid Them

Steering through the credit card maze can get complicated, especially if you're beginning. Let's break down the usual credit card traps and demonstrate how to dodge them:

- **Minimum monthly payment:** This one's a slow burner. Paying only the minimum monthly can drag out your debt and pile up interest. Think of it like a video game—paying the minimum is like barely scraping through a level. You want to aim higher to conquer your debt faster.
- **0% interest offers:** These are like the free trials of the credit card world. They're great initially, but the interest rate can skyrocket when the trial ends (usually after 6 to 12 months). Always check what the rate will be post-trial.
- **Deferred interest:** It's like a ticking time bomb. Remember, while you might not have to pay interest during the promotional period, failing to pay off your balance before it ends fully means you'll face all the interest that's been adding up.
- **Cash advances:** Think of cash advances as a convenience with a cost. They come with high interest (sometimes 20-30%) that accumulates immediately, plus a fee for each withdrawal.
- **Cash and travel bonuses:** These bonuses can tempt you into spending more to "earn" them. It's like getting a small prize for spending a lot. Be smart, and don't spend to get rewards.
- **Changing terms:** Keep your radar on for any alterations in your credit card terms because they may not always be in your favor. Ensure that you regularly review updates from your credit card provider. Stay vigilant!

- **Points and bonuses:** They're like carrots dangled in front of you. Great if they align with your spending, but don't let them dictate your purchases.
- **Multiple fees:** These can add up from annual to late payment fees. It's like paying extra for a game you already own. Keep an eye on these and consider cards with lower fee structures.

Avoiding these traps is all about staying informed and making intelligent choices. Keep track of your spending, pay more than the minimum, and always read the fine print.

DEBT MANAGEMENT

Debt means you owe money to someone else. Think of it as a handy tool that lets you buy things or make investments that might be too expensive for you right now. But remember, it's super important to manage it wisely to avoid any trouble.

When you take out a loan or use a credit card to borrow money, you commit to paying back the borrowed amount, often with some extra interest added on top. If you handle this responsibility wisely, it can be an intelligent way to build your credit gradually. However, it's crucial to remember that this arrangement comes with risks for you and the lender.

As a young person, you face significant debt risks, and it's easy to rack up, especially using credit cards. This can get overwhelming and even more challenging if something unpredictable occurs, like losing your employment. For instance, a study by Demos titled "Generation Broke" found that debt among 18–24-year-olds had risen dramatically, with this age group spending a significant portion of their income (30%) on debt payments (Gensheimer,

2005). Credit card companies often target college students with tempting offers, which usually leads to significant credit card debt.

The effects can stretch far and wide if you don't manage debt well. It might hold you back from big life goals like getting your own house or starting a family, all because of the financial strain. This is especially tough for students facing these challenges. The Federal Reserve Bank of New York found a high delinquency rate among student borrowers, indicating a struggle to manage educational debt (Weissmann, 2012). This doesn't only affect your finances; it also has broader implications for the economy. When young adults struggle with high levels of student debt, joining or remaining in the middle class becomes more challenging.

Furthermore, the effects of debt aren't limited to just young adults. Older age groups are also increasingly burdened by debt, especially educational loans, as they return to school for new skills in a challenging job market. However, this investment doesn't always pay off, leading to financial strain across multiple age groups.

The key takeaway is the importance of financial literacy and understanding how to manage debt responsibly. Whether it's through formal education or learning from family and personal experiences, knowing how to handle credit and debt is crucial to avoid the potential pitfalls that come with it.

Strategies for Managing Existing Debt and Avoiding Excessive Obligation

To handle your debt and stay away from debt you don't need, it's crucial to have an intelligent plan. Let's explore some fundamental approaches that can help you:

- **Assess your current debts:** Begin by clearly viewing your debts. List down all the debts you presently have. Jot down the amount you owe for each debt, the interest rates, and how much you pay each month. This step will help you fully understand your financial situation.
- **Make a budget:** Create a realistic budget that matches your income and expenses. Don't forget to include your debt payments. By doing this, you're taking charge of your money, ensuring you can handle your debts, and managing your finances like a pro.
- **Track your spending:** Ensure you're keeping a keen watch on your daily spending. This helps you figure out where your money is going. Doing this lets you spot places to trim down and save some cash.
- **Earn more money:** Consider boosting your income by picking up a part-time job, selling stuff you no longer use, or taking on some freelance gigs.
- **Stop using your credit cards:** To prevent accumulating more debt, limit your credit card use. If necessary, leave your cards at home to avoid impulsive spending.
- **Change debt-enabling habits:** Identify and change habits that contribute to your debt. This might include dining out less, cutting back on expensive hobbies, or avoiding sales and promotions that encourage unnecessary spending.
- **Reduce your debt load:** You can make this happen using different methods:

  o **Balance transfer credit cards:** Move your debt with high interest to a card offering a lower interest rate at the start. But remember to check out any fees for transferring balances and the interest rate once that initial period is over.

○ **Consolidation loans:** You can use personal loans to merge your debts. Lenders usually offer these loans with a set interest rate and a clear deadline for you to pay them back. This means you'll have a clear strategy for settling your debt within a defined period.

○ **Home equity loans:** This option is for homeowners, but be cautious as it puts your home at risk.

○ **Snowball or avalanche methods:** You've got two methods to choose from when tackling your debts: the snowball and the avalanche methods. The snowball method is about starting with your smaller debts and working on them first. On the other hand, the avalanche method zeroes in on paying off the debts with the highest interest rates. It's all about finding the strategy that works best for you!

- **Seek professional help:** If you need improvement, consider contacting nonprofit credit counseling organizations or financial advisors. They're there to provide you with tailored guidance, help you create plans to manage your debt, and offer support in managing your budget.

Always remember that effectively handling and cutting down on debt requires discipline, careful planning, and, in some cases, getting expert advice. Each move you make to pay down your debt brings you one step closer to achieving financial freedom.

EXAMPLES OF TEENAGERS' STORIES OF CREDIT MANAGEMENT

Meet Alex, 17, who got a credit card but played it smart. Instead of splurging, Alex used it for small, essential purchases and paid each month's total balance. This intelligent move helped Alex avoid interest charges and the dreaded debt trap. By monitoring spending through a budgeting app, Alex stayed within his limits and built a good credit score. It wasn't always easy, especially with friends' flashy buys, but Alex knew the importance of financial health, setting a solid foundation for the future. And the best part? No huge debt to worry about!

17-year-old Jordan got a credit card and felt on top of the world. Initially, it was just about small treats—a game and a fancy meal. But soon, it became a habit. The thrill of swiping the card overshadowed the reality of mounting bills. Jordan missed payment deadlines, accruing high interest. It hit hard when a denied card at the checkout brought the stark truth crashing down. Burdened with debt and a damaged credit score, Jordan realized that with significant spending power comes great responsibility—a harsh but invaluable lesson in financial management.

Meet Sarah, a vibrant 18-year-old teenage girl who got her first credit card. At first, it felt like a ticket to freedom. She used it for shopping sprees, dining out with friends, and even a weekend getaway. But the excitement soon turned into anxiety as the bills started piling up. Interest charges began to eat into her savings, and she realized she was in over her head. Sarah decided to open up to her parents who didn't scold her but offered guidance. She created a budget with their support, learned about responsible credit card use, and gradually paid off her debt. She learned a harsh lesson, which molded her into a financially intelligent young woman.

Lily got her first credit card and a student loan for college. Initially, it felt like a dream come true—shopping, attending parties, and having exciting college adventures. But soon, she lost track of her spending, maxed out her credit card, and used her student loan for non-educational expenses. Her debt snowballed, and she realized the gravity of her situation. Lily sought financial guidance, learned about budgeting, and worked part-time to repay her debts. It was a challenging journey, but she emerged wiser, vowing to use credit responsibly and make the most of her education.

These stories teach teenagers important lessons about responsibly managing credit:

- **Alex's smart spending:** Alex's story teaches us the power of intelligent spending. Alex avoided the debt trap by using a credit card for small, essential purchases and paying the entire monthly balance. The key takeaway here is only to use credit when necessary and ensure you can pay it off promptly to avoid interest charges.
- **Jordan's cautionary tale:** Look at Jordan's story; it's a warning we can all learn from. Using your credit card impulsively and frequently can quickly pile up bills and interest charges. The message here is crystal clear: Watch how you spend and stay on top of those payment deadlines to keep debt from getting out of hand.
- **Sarah's openness and guidance:** Sarah's story highlights the importance of seeking help. Her credit card bills became overwhelming, so she asked her parents for guidance. Their support, budgeting, and responsible credit card use helped her overcome the challenge. It emphasizes that it's okay to ask for assistance and that parents can be valuable allies in financial matters.
- **Lily's debt management:** Lily's experience with a credit card and a student loan demonstrates how easy it is to misuse credit when not used for its intended purpose. She took charge of her financial responsibility by seeking financial advice, educating herself about budgeting, and

diligently working towards paying off her debts. The takeaway is that using loans and credit responsibly is crucial, especially for educational purposes.

These stories underscore the importance of responsible credit card and loan usage. They emphasize the need to

- spend wisely, especially on essential items.
- steer clear of interest fees, making sure to ultimately pay off your credit card balances.
- stay mindful of your spending habits and avoid making impulsive purchases.
- seek guidance and support from parents or financial advisors when facing economic challenges.
- use loans and credit for their intended purposes, such as education.

By learning from these stories, you can make informed financial decisions, build good credit habits, and avoid the pitfalls of irresponsible credit usage.

CREDIT CARD RESPONSIBILITY CHECKLIST

Now that you're a member of the credit-earning community, you should know some fundamental things. Building and keeping a good credit score requires time and effort, which can be delicate. Your credit score can decrease rapidly, but it needs time to improve. So, beginning your credit journey in the best way possible is vital. No need to worry! Here are five crucial steps to keep in mind:

- **Repay your balance monthly:** Remember there's a crucial rule for credit cards: Pay off your entire balance each month. Following this rule, you avoid paying extra interest fees and build a track record of using credit responsibly. This isn't just beneficial for you; it's also a strategy to enhance your credit score!

- **Stay within your credit limit:** Credit cards have a set credit limit, especially for beginners, to keep you from spending too much. It's essential to stay within this limit and not go over it. Exceeding it can damage your credit score and result in additional fees.
- **Set up a payment schedule:** Plan when you'll pay off your credit card each month and stick to it. Consistency is critical in managing your credit effectively. You can use tools like Central Bank Online and mobile banking to keep track of your finances, set up account alerts, use money manager features, and even pay your bills online.
- **Regularly check your credit report:** After putting in all that hard work, seeing the results is crucial. You should periodically check your credit report to ensure everything is on track. Aim to review your credit report at least yearly. You can use free online tools like Annual Credit Report to access it. Just remember to use trustworthy websites when you check your credit report.
- **Enjoy the rewards:** Certain credit cards sweeten the deal by giving you rewards when you use them. These rewards can be pretty tempting, but picking a rewards program that matches your lifestyle and spending patterns is crucial. Keep in mind that rewards differ, so make sure to research and discover the one that fits you perfectly.

Think of building and keeping a solid credit score as a financial marathon. It demands discipline, responsibility, and an intelligent plan. By sticking to these five steps, you'll be on your path to creating a reliable credit history and enjoying the rewards of using credit responsibly. Remember, this is a journey. The earlier you kickstart it, the brighter your financial future will glow.

KEY TAKEAWAYS

- Credit cards are like loans with interest, not free money.
- Credit means you borrow money now and pay it back later, and having good credit is critical to achieving financial success.
- Credit scores represent how well you handle borrowed money and can affect loan interest rates, housing, and job opportunities.
- Responsible credit use starts with simple steps like getting a savings account, becoming an authorized user, or using a secured credit card.
- To construct a substantial credit history, settle your bills promptly and keep your credit utilization below 30%.
- Keep a close eye on your credit score and regularly review your credit report to ensure everything is accurate.
- Managing debt requires assessing your current debts, budgeting, tracking spending, and exploring debt reduction strategies.
- Seeking professional help and understanding the risks of debt are crucial.

Let's step it up! Now that you've got the hang of handling credit cards and keeping debt in check, it's the perfect moment to aim high. Turning your dreams into reality hinges on setting and achieving financial goals. So, let's jump into the next phase and explore how you can turn those dreams into actual achievements!

CHAPTER THREE

SETTING AND ACHIEVING FINANCIAL GOALS

Imagine you just got $10,000! Pretty awesome. Now, think about what you'd do with it. This isn't just about spending money; it's a sneak peek into how you handle finances. Your choices now can give you a hint about your money smarts in the future. So, how do you go about it?

TECHNIQUES FOR GOAL SETTING

Effective financial management involves utilizing SMART goals, and in this discussion, we will explore the concept of SMART goals and how to apply them to maintain economic control:

- **Specific:** You should establish clear and specific goals for a precise target. For instance, instead of stating, "Money should be saved by me," you can express, "I intend to set aside $300 for a new gaming console." This technique ensures an unmistakable awareness of your objective.
- **Measurable:** Ensure your goals have clear measures to help you to monitor your advancement. When saving for a

gaming console, record the amount you save weekly or monthly. This will help maintain your motivation and indicate your proximity to achieving your goal. Make sure that you have practical and feasible plans.

- **Achievable:** Setting achievable and sensible objectives is necessary. Challenging yourself while remaining honest about what you can realistically achieve is essential. For instance, if you earn a modest income from a part-time job, saving $1,000 monthly might be a difficult target, but saving $300 for a few months could be within your reach.
- **Relevant:** Select goals that hold significance to you and are in harmony with your overall financial plans. If you intend to pursue a college education, consider setting a savings goal for tuition.
- **Time-bound:** Set a deadline for your goal. A specific timeframe keeps you focused and motivates you to stick to your plan—like "I will save $300 for the gaming console by June."

A recent survey found that 93% of teens believe financial knowledge is essential for achieving life goals. Yet, the average National Financial Literacy Test score was only 64% (*Survey Finds*, 2022). Establishing SMART goals can be a practical method for enhancing financial literacy and boosting self-assurance.

How to Identify Personal Financial Goals

First, break down your financial goals into three categories: short-term, medium-term, and longer-term. Short-term goals include setting aside funds for a new phone or purchasing a concert ticket. Medium-term goals include saving for a car or college expenses. Longer-term goals are more about building a solid financial foundation for your future, like saving for a house or retirement.

Creating a budget is an excellent initial step, as it involves comprehending the inflow and outflow of your finances. You should monitor your income, which may come from sources like a part-time job, allowance, or birthday gifts, as well as your expenditures, encompassing items such as your Netflix subscription or snacks with friends. Budgeting apps can enhance this process, making it more engaging and interactive for users.

Opening a savings account can be your next step. It's about storing your money and understanding how interest works. Imagine your money growing over time by generating more money.

Investing might sound like something only adults do, but it's never too early. Investing can involve purchasing stocks of companies you have an affinity for or have faith in. This is where you can learn about risk and how the stock market works.

An emergency fund is critical. Life is unpredictable—your phone might break or you might need to buy something unexpectedly. Setting aside money for these situations can save you from stress and debt.

Speaking of debt, try to use it as little as possible. Getting caught up with credit cards and loans is easy but can lead to financial challenges if not managed wisely.

Building credit is also essential. You might not be thinking about big purchases like a car or a home now, but having a good credit score will be vital when you do. You can start by becoming an authorized user on a parent's credit card or getting a low-limit card for small purchases you can pay off monthly.

Another crucial step in the college application process is seeking financial aid. Researching scholarships, grants, and loans early on and applying for as many as possible will substantially lower your education expenses.

These steps are just the beginning. Remember, financial literacy isn't just about saving money; it's about making informed decisions that affect your current and future economic health. Despite the importance of financial literacy, it's often overlooked in school curriculums, leaving many of you to learn from your parents or self-educate. So, take advantage of resources like financial literacy courses, apps, and even family discussions about money to enhance your understanding and skills.

Always remember that your choices today can significantly impact your financial future. Ensure you create a plan outlining how to achieve your economic objectives.

CREATING A PLAN TO ACHIEVE GOALS

A financial plan is paramount for teenagers wanting to ensure their financial future. Here's a step-by-step guide based on the latest research and statistics to help you reach your financial goals:

- **Set financial goals:** Start by identifying your short-term and long-term financial goals. Whether saving for college, buying a car, or having extra cash for emergencies, clear goals will help you stay focused.
- **Track your money:** Understanding where you spend your money is crucial. A survey found that 62% of teens use mobile or online applications for money management, a significant increase from 48% in 2019 (Harley, 2022). This habit can help you monitor your spending and savings effectively.
- **Budget for emergencies:** Life is unpredictable. More than two-thirds of teens (69%) say that rising education costs have affected their plans for additional education after high school (Harley, 2022). Spending money regularly can

help you control unexpected expenses and prevent them from disrupting your financial goals.

- **Tackle high-interest debt:** If you have any debt, especially high-interest ones like credit card debts, prioritize paying them off. It's one of the most practical efforts to achieve financial freedom.
- **Plan for retirement:** Though retirement might seem far off, an early start can have a considerable impact. Compound interest can increase the value of even modest savings over time.
- **Optimize your finances with tax planning:** Understanding how taxes affect your income and savings is crucial. Seek advice from parents or financial advisors to learn more about this.
- **Invest to build your future goals:** With 27% of kids investing in cryptocurrency and 28% in stocks as of 2021, it's clear that teenagers are already taking steps towards investing (*Teenage Money Management*, n.d.). However, ensure you understand the risks and start with safer investments.
- **Grow your financial well-being:** Financial well-being isn't just about having money; it's also about feeling secure and making choices that make you happy. Learning about financial management now can set you up for a lifetime of well-being.
- **Estate planning:** While it might seem too early to think about this, understanding the basics of estate planning, like wills and how to manage assets, is a good practice for long-term financial planning.

Remember, the financial landscape is ever-changing. Thus, staying informed and adapting your financial plan over time is crucial to building a solid financial foundation that will support you through all stages of life.

The Importance of Persistence and Flexibility in Goal Setting and Achievement

Setting and achieving goals as a teenager can be a transformative experience, shaping your future success and personal development. For a compelling journey, it's essential to have two key qualities: the ability to persist and the capacity to adapt.

Persistence: Your Powerhouse

Persistence is the steadfast pursuit of your goals, especially when facing challenges. Imagine you're learning to play the guitar. At first, it feels impossible—your fingers ache, and the chords sound off. But with persistent practice, you gradually improve. The essence of persistence lies in overcoming challenges and refusing to quit. Research has shown that effort, a key component of persistence, is vital in reaching your goals (Kazdin, 2018). Every setback presents a chance for learning and personal growth. By focusing on the process and not just the outcome, you build a strong foundation for future achievements. This approach to persistence is like the story of the tortoise and the hare, where consistent effort leads to success, even if it's not immediate.

Flexibility: Your Secret Weapon

Flexibility is about adapting to changes and thinking creatively about your goals. You aim to become a great basketball player, but an injury sidelines you. Instead of giving up, you shift focus temporarily to studying game strategies or improving your diet. This adaptability is flexibility in action. It's about coping with changes and adjusting your goals when necessary. Being flexible doesn't mean abandoning your goals but finding different paths.

Setting SMART Goals

One practical approach to balancing persistence and flexibility involves establishing SMART goals. SMART is an acronym for Specific, Measurable, Achievable, Realistic, and Time-bound. This technique guarantees that your plans are well-defined and feasible within a designated timeframe, enabling you to maintain focus and adapt when necessary.

The Function of Visual Aids and Regular Check-Ins

To keep your goals in sight, use visual aids like vision boards or goal-setting apps. These tools can serve as constant reminders of what you're working towards. Regular check-ins on your progress are also crucial. They help you celebrate small victories and reassess your approach if you're not advancing as planned.

NOTE 1: You can check Teen Mag's guide for creating vision boards.

URL: https://www.theteenmagazine.com/the-ultimate-guide-to-building-your-dream-vision-board

NOTE 2: You can download Mint from Google Play or the App Store if you want to try a goal-setting app.

Parental Support and Independence

As a teenager, your independence in goal setting is crucial. While parental support is essential, your goals should be self-driven. Parents can encourage this independence by asking open-ended questions and providing feedback focused on effort rather than outcomes. This approach helps set realistic goals, boosts your confidence, and reinforces the importance of perseverance.

Embracing Growth Mindset

A growth mindset, where you believe in developing your abilities through effort, is fundamental to achieving goals. This mindset enables you to regard barriers as stepping stones, transforming challenges into opportunities for personal growth.

Your journey towards achieving goals as a teenager is both challenging and rewarding. You can succeed by embracing persistence and flexibility, establishing SMART goals, utilizing visual aids, actively seeking parental support, and nurturing a growth mindset. Always remember that achieving success involves attaining your objectives and developing skills, resilience, and self-awareness throughout your journey.

REAL STORIES OF TEEN SUCCESS

Sanil Chawla

Let's talk about Sanil Chawla, a real go-getter who turned his challenges into success. In high school, Sanil hit a roadblock while starting a web design company—he needed a guardian's signature for everything! He did not easily give up, so he created Hack+, an innovation for young businesspeople. This nonprofit helps teens navigate the tricky world of legal and financial stuff in business. Thanks to his perseverance and innovative thinking, Sanil made things easier for others and earned a spot on Forbes' 30 Under 30 list (*Forbes 30*, n.d.). His journey shows you can turn obstacles into stepping stones with persistence and adaptability.

Erik Finman

Erik Finman took a path less traveled. He invested $1,000 in Bitcoin when he was 12, and by 18, he became a millionaire! When school felt more like a drag than a journey, Erik bet his parents he'd make a million before college. He won, big time. But his story doesn't stop at Bitcoin. Erik founded Botangle, a learning platform, at just 15 (Aydin, 2020). Later, he sold it for even more Bitcoin. Today, Erik's not just sitting on his success; he's flying high, investing in aircraft. His story is more than just about money; it's about taking risks and following your passions, even when they're not the usual path.

Alex Koch

As a kid, Alex began saving at his local credit union. Once he hit $1,000, he smartly moved to a CD. His teen years saw him managing a checking account and getting a secured credit card at 18. With his first job, he even started an IRA. Now 25 years old and working in construction, Alex is a pro-saver with a fantastic credit score of over 800 and $60,000 saved up for his first home (Carosa, 2021). For Alex, saving is just a slice of life! Consider opening a Certificate of Deposit (CD) when you've saved a decent sum. It offers better interest rates and encourages long-term saving. Moreover, start an Individual Retirement Account (IRA) early as Alex did. It's a secure way to save for your future.

Practical Tips and Strategies Used by Successful Teens

Let's dive into some practical tips and strategies inspired by the incredible stories of Sanil Chawla, Erik Finman, and Alex Koch. These determined individuals have demonstrated that one can transform their aspirations into tangible achievements with the right mindset and proactive efforts.

Start early and save smart

- Just like Alex, start saving as early as possible. Even small amounts can grow over time.
- Research various savings accounts and select one that meets your distinct needs. Effective money management serves as the initial stride toward achieving financial success.

Embrace entrepreneurship

- If you possess a business idea, don't allow your age and other obstacles to hinder your progress. Sanil's story shows that you can create solutions to your challenges.
- Explore entrepreneurship programs or platforms like Hack+ that can guide you through the legal and financial aspects of starting a business.
- Take calculated risks just as Erik did with Bitcoin. Innovation frequently arises from unconventional thinking and the courage to stand out.

Persevere through challenges

- Challenges are part of any journey. Don't give up when things get tough.
- Learn from setbacks like Erik did when he faced obstacles in school. Your greatest assets are adaptability and resilience.
- Stay focused on the ultimate objective as success favors those who persevere through challenges.

Invest for the future

- Explore investment opportunities, even if you're young. Erik's Bitcoin investment proved that intelligent choices can yield incredible returns.
- Diversify your investments. Consider cryptocurrencies, stocks, or real estate as Erik diversified beyond Bitcoin.

Educate yourself

- Invest time learning new skills just as Erik did when he founded Botangle.
- Remain curious and receptive to fresh experiences and actively search for educational materials that resonate with your interests.
- Explore online courses, workshops, and mentorship opportunities to expand your knowledge.

Network and seek guidance

- Connect with mentors and like-minded individuals who can provide guidance and support like Sanil did in the entrepreneurial world.
- Participate in networking activities or join online societies that align with your interests or objectives.
- Don't hesitate to seek assistance or guidance from others as numerous accomplished individuals are ready to share their insights and experiences.

These practical tips and strategies can set you on the path to success just like Sanil Chawla, Erik Finman, and Alex Koch. Remember that your journey may have obstacles, but with determination and the right approach, you can turn those obstacles into stepping stones toward your goals.

FINANCIAL GOALS REFLECTION QUESTIONS

Here are 20 reflective questions with explanations on why they matter and how they align with your values, designed to help you think deeply about your financial goals:

1. What are your short-term financial goals for the next year? (e.g., saving for a new phone)

- **Why it matters:** Short-term goals allow you to fulfill immediate desires or needs, like upgrading your tech, which can improve your daily life.

2. Why does achieving these short-term goals matter to you personally?

- **Why it matters:** Recognizing the personal importance of these objectives can inspire motivation and cultivate a sense of purpose.

3. What are your long-term financial aspirations, like saving for college or a dream home?

- **Why it matters:** Long-term goals set the stage for your future and provide a sense of direction and accomplishment.

4. How do these long-term goals align with your core values and beliefs?

- **Why it matters:** Aligning goals with your values ensures that your financial journey reflects what's important to you.

5. Are your financial goals specific and measurable or vague and undefined?

- **Why it matters:** Clear, measurable goals help you track progress and stay focused. Frustration and uncertainty can arise from having unclear objectives.

6. What steps can you take today to begin working toward your financial objectives?

- **Why it matters:** Taking small actions at this moment can result in significant accomplishments in the future.

7. How comfortable are you with budgeting and tracking your expenses?

- **Why it matters:** Budgeting is the foundation of attaining monetary success, enabling effective money management by actively tracking expenses.

8. Have you considered seeking guidance from a financial advisor or mentor?

- **Why it matters:** Learning from experts or mentors can offer practical wisdom and help you to make educated decisions.

9. Do you know the likely benefits of compound interest in long-term savings?

- **Why it matters:** Compound interest can turbocharge your savings and investments over time, building wealth steadily.

10. How does an emergency fund help your financial security?

- **Why it matters:** An emergency fund offers a financial safety cushion, helping you prepare for unforeseen expenses or emergencies.

11. How do your financial goals contribute to your overall well-being and happiness?

- **Why it matters:** Attaining financial security and accomplishing one's goals can enhance mental and emotional well-being, ultimately contributing to a more joyful existence.

12. What sacrifices or changes can you make to attain your financial objectives?

- **Why it matters:** Achieving significant goals often requires trade-offs or adjustments in your spending habits.

13. Have you thought about diversifying your investments to reduce risk?

- **Why it matters:** Diversifying your investments spreads risk and can shield them from market fluctuations.

14. Are you open to adjusting your goals as your life circumstances change?

- **Why it matters:** Flexibility in goal-setting allows you to adapt to evolving life situations and stay on track.

15. How do you intend to maintain motivation and monitor your advancement in achieving your financial objectives?

- **Why it matters:** Motivation and tracking are essential for maintaining focus and celebrating achievements.

16. What role do education and continuous learning play in your financial journey?

- **Why it matters:** Continuous learning gives you the wisdom and skills to make informed monetary decisions.

17. How can you incorporate philanthropy or giving back into your financial goals?

- **Why it matters:** Including charitable giving aligns your goals with values of generosity and social responsibility.

18. Are you prepared to handle unexpected financial setbacks or windfalls?

- **Why it matters:** Being ready for financial surprises ensures you can navigate challenges and opportunities.

19. How will you celebrate your financial achievements along the way?

- **Why it matters:** Celebrating milestones boosts motivation and makes your financial journey more enjoyable.

20. How can inflation affect your long-term savings objectives?

- **Why it matters:** Inflation gradually diminishes the buying power of money, making it crucial to factor it into your savings strategies.

Reflecting on these questions and their explanations can help you gain clarity, motivation, and purpose in your financial journey. Achieving your goals and constructing a financially secure future aligned with your values is essential.

KEY TAKEAWAYS

- SMART goals are specific, measurable, achievable, relevant, and time-bound, helping you stay focused on your financial objectives.
- Short-term, medium-term, and long-term financial goals are essential for shaping your financial future.
- Practical steps for financial success include setting clear goals, budgeting, and managing emergencies.
- Flexibility and persistence are vital for achieving your goals in a changing world.

Everything you need to realize your financial aspirations is at your fingertips! Establish specific goals, handle money smartly, and gain insights from actual success stories. The next chapter will study the fundamentals of constructing a solid financial base to underpin your life's goals.

CHAPTER FOUR

BUILDING A SOLID FINANCIAL FOUNDATION

I magine facing an unexpected expense out of the blue. Everyone experiences this at some point, and that's fine! But here's the deal: Most teens aren't ready for it. Let's be proactive and build a financial safety net together.

FUNDAMENTAL FINANCIAL CONCEPTS

Let's dive into some key financial concepts in a way that's easy to grasp and relevant to you as a teenager:

- **Income:** This is the money you earn or receive. As a teen, your income might come from different places. It could be assistance from your parents, cash from part-time employment, or even earnings from a side hustle. In 2024, the average American teen earns about $33,000-$38,000 annually, but this can vary based on where you live and your job type (*How Much*, 2023).
- **Expenses:** These are the costs of things you need or want. There are two kinds of expenditures:

○ *Essential expenses* are for items you need, like food or transportation.
○ *Discretionary expenses* include something you like but don't need, like games or going out with friends.

Most teens spend money on clothes, food, video games, and personal care items. Interestingly, teenage girls spend more on clothes and personal care, while boys spend more on video games.

- **Net worth:** This is the discrepancy between what you possess (your assets) and what you owe (your liabilities). For teens, this could mean the difference between the money you have saved and any debts you might have, like money owed to your parents or a credit card.
- **Saving:** Saving money is crucial. Many teens are getting good at it. Studies show that up to 80% of teens are actively saving, which is excellent! The average American teen saves between $548 and $720 annually (Sharpe, 2023). Your savings could go towards big goals like college, a car, or even starting your own business.
- **Budgeting:** It's all about planning how to use your money. Keeping watch of your income and expenses can help you make wiser financial choices. For example, if earning $50 a week from a part-time job, you can save $20, spend $20 on essentials, and use the remaining $10 for fun stuff.

Remember, the financial habits you develop now can impact your future. Being mindful of your spending and saving can set you up for a more stable and stress-free financial life. So, keep track of your money, save for your goals, and spend wisely!

SMART DECISION-MAKING

Making smart financial choices sets the foundation for a stable future for teenagers. It's about understanding the difference between needs and wants and managing your resources smartly. Let's break down some key strategies:

- **Check your finances regularly:** Keeping an eye on your finances at least once a week is crucial. This habit helps you stay vigilant about your spending patterns and financial health. Surprisingly, a recent study showed that 62% of teens now use mobile or online applications for money management, a significant increase from 48% in 2019 (*New Research*, 2022).
- **Use financial tracking software:** In today's digital age, several apps and software tools can help you track your spending and savings. This aligns with the trend of teens increasingly turning to digital solutions for financial management.
- **Create a spending plan:** Create a budget that separates what you need from what you want. Needs include essentials like food, water, shelter, clothing, and safety. Wants include travel, entertainment, video games, designer clothing, junk food, and sports cars. It's crucial to prioritize needs over wants.
- **Set savings goals:** Aim to save a portion of any money you receive, whether from a part-time job, allowance, or gifts. You might save for short-term goals, like purchasing a new game, or long-term objectives, such as building a college fund.
- **Consider professional advice:** Sometimes, seeking guidance from a financial coach or tax strategist is helpful,

especially when planning for significant expenses like college.

- **Focus on numbers, not emotions:** Financial decisions should be based more on logical assessment than emotional impulses. This helps in avoiding unnecessary expenses on things you don't need.

Remember, financial literacy is a crucial skill that can significantly impact your future. As the economic landscape becomes more complex, starting early in educating yourself about making good financial choices is vital. Understanding and practicing these principles will set you up for a more secure and informed financial future.

THE ROLE OF AN EMERGENCY FUND

Think of an emergency fund like your financial superhero: always prepared to come to the rescue when unexpected situations arise. It's like a stash of cash for those "oh no!" moments—the car breaks down, the phone takes a swim, or a surprise dentist visit.

The cool part? Building an emergency fund is about more than just being ready for mishaps. It offers peace of mind and teaches you to be financially savvy. It's all about being prepared so you don't have to stress or go into debt when life throws a curveball.

So, how much should you save? Most folks say to aim for three to six months of essential living expenses (*Emergency Funds*, 2022). But, as a teen, your costs might be different. Consider car payments, phone bills, or even school-related costs. Stay calm if six months' worth seems like a mountain. Starting small is okay. Even a few hundred bucks can be a game-changer.

Now, the fun part is how you build this fund. Begin by establishing a specific objective. How much money are you aiming to save? Then, make a budget to see where your cash is going. This assists you in determining how much you can consistently save.

Next, find an excellent savings account with no fees and an option to earn interest. Set up automatic transfers so saving happens without you even thinking about it. And look for ways to cut back on stuff you don't need. Cutting down on dining out or reducing impulsive purchases brings you one step closer to achieving your goal as each saved dollar adds up toward it.

If you've received additional money from a side gig or birthday gifts, stash it in your emergency fund. Remember, the aim is to increase it steadily over time. Stay patient and committed to your goal.

An emergency fund is all about setting you up for success. It's your financial cushion, allowing you to handle surprises without breaking the bank. Begin today, no matter how modest your start, and witness the growth of your emergency fund.

How to Start and Build an Emergency Fund

Starting and building an emergency fund as a teenager is an intelligent step toward financial independence and security. Here's how you can go about it:

- **Understand the importance:** An emergency fund is a cash reserve for unforeseen situations such as sudden job loss, medical expenses, and car repairs. It's a safety net to prevent debt and teaches you responsible money management.

- **Set clear goals:** Decide how much you want to save. Begin with a modest goal and slowly raise it over time. Saving even a few dollars each week can accumulate over time.
- **Create a budget:** Stay in the know about where your money is going. Create a list of your income sources, be it allowance or part-time job earnings, and maintain a record of all your spending. Doing this will provide a clear view of your monthly savings potential.
- **Open a savings account:** Choose an account separate from your everyday spending. Look for ones with no minimum balance, no monthly fees, and a decent interest rate to help your savings grow.
- **Automate your savings:** Set up automatic transfers from your checking to your savings account to make saving effortless, allowing you to set money aside quickly.
- **Reduce unnecessary expenses:** Identify categories where you can cut expenses, like dining out less frequently or curbing impulsive buys. Each dollar you save can go to your emergency fund.
- **Earn extra money:** Seek chances to earn extra money. Babysitting, selling unused items, or taking on odd jobs can help increase your emergency fund.
- **Be patient and stay committed:** Constructing an emergency fund requires dedication and self-control. Avoid the urge to dip into these savings for non-urgent purposes.
- **Track your progress:** Regularly check your savings growth and adjust your budget and goals. Celebrating small milestones can be motivating.
- **Use wisely:** Remember, this fund is for emergencies, like a sudden phone repair or medical expense, not for regular spending or wants.

By following these steps, you'll build a financial safety net and develop essential money management skills that will benefit you in the long run.

REAL-LIFE SUCCESS STORIES

Katherine: How Her Savings Made Her Realize Her Dream

Like many teenagers, Katherine viewed her bank account as a way to enjoy life's pleasures, such as trendy clothes and fancy daily coffees. She had no long-term financial goals and was influenced by her parents, who could have been better with money. Katherine lived for the moment, spending without thinking about the future. On the other hand, her friends always discussed saving, something she found unnecessary until an unexpected situation arose.

When her friends planned a last-minute snowboarding trip to Japan, Katherine was shocked to realize she had no savings for such spontaneous adventures or plans. This was a turning point. She started saving diligently for the trip and her future self, who had bigger aspirations. It became satisfying for her to see her savings grow.

However, life threw Katherine a curveball. While driving to work, she had a car accident and lost her job since she couldn't use her damaged car. To make matters worse, she needed surgery and had no health insurance. Her savings rescued her, enabling her to maintain financial stability during this challenging time.

Recovering from surgery and bedridden, Katherine had time to reflect on her life. She realized she hadn't pursued her true passions. The savings Katherine had accumulated offered her the security to explore new paths. She discovered her talent in art, created a portfolio, and started selling her work online.

She began earning from her art in six months, fulfilling a dream she had overlooked. Katherine's story is a powerful reminder to teenagers about the importance of saving. It's about preparing for emergencies and allowing yourself to chase your dreams.

Haley Persichitte: Small Steps Make a Big Difference

Haley Persichitte, a vibrant 24-year-old from Denver, is about staying fit and healthy. She's committed to her fitness regime, investing in Barry's Bootcamp and CorePower Yoga and keeping up with her ClassPass subscription. Besides working out, Haley has her hands full with financial responsibilities like her monthly car payment and rent. But that doesn't hinder her from savoring life. She loves catching up with friends over dinner, a perfect way to unwind.

Even without a college degree, Haley's doing well for herself. She's a house manager for a nearby family, a job that she's good at. What's impressive is her knack for saving money. She sets aside about $600 monthly, primarily for unforeseen expenses. Thanks to her intelligent saving habits, she's already got about $15,000 in her savings account. However, she's feeling the pinch with the rising food and gas costs, making it harder to save as much as she used to.

One thing Haley has yet to think much about is saving for retirement. It's not on her radar now, but that's common at her age. For young people like Haley, the future can seem far away, but it's never too early to start thinking about it. Remember that taking small steps today can result in significant transformations in the future. Keep rocking it, Haley, and maybe consider retirement savings—it could be your next big goal!

Thea Pham: Helps Her Vietnamese Family but Saves for Retirement

Thea Pham, a 27-year-old first-generation Vietnamese immigrant living in Los Angeles with her husband, has a challenging but rewarding financial journey. Working in finance, Thea earns a significant salary, typically between $160,000 to $250,000 annually, though she can't share the exact amount due to job regulations. Despite her high income, Thea faces unique financial responsibilities compared to her peers.

A large portion of her earnings goes back to her family in Vietnam. She grew up with this cultural expectation and continues to honor it, even though it's pretty different from what many Americans do. Thea admits that this commitment means she can't always spend freely like her friends with similar incomes.

Aside from supporting her family, Thea also contributes to her household expenses. Her husband's income primarily covers their living and housing costs, and Thea pitches in with up to 20% of these expenses. Whatever she has left, she wisely invests in retirement and savings accounts. She's also ready to help out when relatives need financial assistance and enjoys spending on travel occasionally.

Thea not only focuses on finance but also boasts a TikTok following of more than 450,000 dedicated followers. There, she shares content about mental health issues, showing her commitment to helping others and raising awareness on important topics.

Despite her financial stability, Thea's life is a blend of fulfilling familial duties and managing her personal and professional growth. Her story is an inspiring example for teenagers, showcasing the importance of balancing cultural values, financial responsibilities, and personal passions.

Lessons Learned From the Stories of Others

Let's break down the valuable lessons we can learn from the stories of Katherine, Haley, and Thea. These stories aren't just fantastic anecdotes but real-life lessons wrapped in experiences.

- **Start saving early:** Katherine's story is like a wake-up call. She shows us the power of saving. You never know when you might want to join an epic snowboarding trip or face an unexpected challenge. Saving isn't just about being ready for emergencies; it's about giving yourself options and freedom in the future. Begin saving regularly, even if it's just a small amount. Over time, those savings accumulate!
- **Pursue your passions**: Lying in bed recovering, Katherine realized life's too short not to do what you love. When she started exploring art, a hidden passion, it opened new doors for her. The lesson? Don't wait for a life-changing moment to chase your dreams. Start now, explore what you love, and who knows where it might lead!
- **Small steps in saving make a big difference:** Haley's story is all about the power of consistent saving. She puts aside $600 each month and look where it got her—a pretty impressive savings account. It's like building a Lego masterpiece: one small piece at a time leads to something unique. Remember that starting with any amount is fine, no matter how small.
- **Plan for the future:** Even though Haley's rocking it with her savings, retirement planning still needs to be added to her radar. But here's the thing: thinking about the long-term future is super important, even when young. Start considering things like retirement savings early. It's one of those things that's easy to put off but super important.

- **Balance personal values and financial responsibilities:**
  Thea's story blends cultural values and financial wisdom.
  She supports her family back in Vietnam, a significant
  cultural responsibility, while also managing her finances
  smartly. She invests in retirement and savings. It shows us
  that you can honor your roots and be financially savvy at
  the same time.
- **Invest in yourself:** Beyond her financial commitments,
  Thea actively dedicates time to her passions, such as
  managing her TikTok channel on mental health topics.
  This teaches us to invest not just in savings or retirement
  but in our personal growth and interests. You've got
  talents and interests—explore them!

Each of these stories is a treasure trove of wisdom. There's much
to learn from Katherine, Haley, and Thea, whether starting to save
early, pursuing your passions, planning for the future, balancing
cultural and financial responsibilities, or investing in yourself.
Consider the valuable lessons from their experiences and apply
them to your financial journey. Your financial future is under your
control—make it remarkable!

FINANCIAL HEALTH CHECK-UP WORKSHEET

Are you ready to evaluate your financial health? This worksheet is
your essential tool, like a check-up for your finances! Let's explore
crucial aspects of assessing your financial status and pinpointing
areas for improvement. Remember, there's no judgment here. We
aim to encourage positive changes!

Income tracking

- How much money do you make monthly?
- Do you earn money from sources other than your primary income, such as working part-time, receiving allowances, or getting gifts?

Understanding your income is step one. Knowing what you get is crucial, whether from a part-time job, allowance, or birthday money.

Expenses breakdown

- List all your monthly expenses (like phone bills, entertainment, and snacks).
- Can you cut down or remove any of your costs?

Expenses can catch you off guard, so keeping tabs on them is vital to understanding where your money flows. You might be splurging excessively on video games or indulgent coffee.

Savings check

- Do you save a portion of your income? How much?
- If not, what's stopping you?

Starting a regular savings habit, even with a small amount, can result in substantial growth over time. If you haven't already, consider starting a savings routine.

Debt awareness

- Do you owe money to anyone, such as borrowing money from friends or family?

- What's your strategy for repaying it?

Owing money is common, but a plan to pay it back is vital. It shows responsibility and keeps your relationships stress-free.

Financial goals setting

- What are your short-term financial goals (like buying a new game or a concert ticket)?
- What about long-term goals (like saving for college or a car)?

Establishing goals provides a clear purpose for your money, making it thrilling to set aside funds for something you desire!

Budgeting basics

- Have you tried creating a budget?
- If you've tried making a budget, does it suit your needs? If you need help, what's preventing you from making it work?

Budgeting isn't exclusive to adults. Mastering money management paves the way for a more prosperous financial future.

Emergency fund insight

- Do you have money for unexpected expenses (like a broken phone)?
- How can you start building this fund?

Life is full of surprises and having some money for those "just in case" moments is super important.

Investment curiosity

- Have you heard about investments (like stocks or savings bonds)?
- Are you excited to learn more about them?

Investing can appear complicated, but it's a fantastic method to increase your wealth gradually. Gaining knowledge at a young age is always a valuable pursuit!

Credit knowledge

- Do you understand the concept of credit and why it holds significance?
- Are you eager to discover how to establish a positive credit history?

Good credit is like a financial report card for adults. Understanding it early can help you a lot in the future.

Money attitude reflection

- How do you feel about money in general?
- Does your attitude towards money affect how you handle it?

Your attitude towards money has a significant impact on how you handle it. Being aware of your attitude helps in making smarter money choices.

How did you do? Remember, this check-up is a starting point. It's all about growing and learning. Keep exploring, stay curious, and you'll be on your way to excellent financial health!

KEY TAKEAWAYS

- Income tracking is essential for understanding your monthly earnings from various sources like jobs, allowances, or gifts.
- Expenses should be categorized into essential (needs) and discretionary (wants), focusing on reducing unnecessary spending.
- Saving money is crucial, and numerous teenagers are actively saving for upcoming objectives such as college or purchasing a car.
- Budgeting involves planning the use of money and balancing savings, essential spending, and leisure activities.
- Regular financial check-ups, at least once a week, help maintain awareness of spending patterns and overall economic health.
- Crafting a budget allows you to distinguish between necessities and desires, prioritizing essential spending.
- Setting clear savings goals, even small ones, can accumulate significantly over time.
- Financial decisions should be based on logic rather than emotions to avoid unnecessary expenses.
- An emergency fund serves as a financial safety cushion for unforeseen circumstances, and it should encompass the cost of essential expenses for a period ranging from three to six months.

You've mastered budgeting and saving—awesome! Now, imagine turning that hard-earned cash into even more. The next chapter will dive into smart investing and earning strategies. Get ready to grow your money and amplify your financial game.

YOUR THOUGHTS MATTER... AND THEY CAN MAKE A BIG DIFFERENCE TO ANOTHER TEEN

"The key factor that will determine your financial future is not the economy; the key factor is your philosophy."

JIM ROHN

In the introduction, I mentioned that money skills aren't just an option for teens; they're a must. The reason is simple: in a couple of years (or perhaps this very year), you will start making financial decisions that will have a powerful impact on everything from when you can buy a home to how much you earn. Being money savvy is one of the key differences between barely making ends meet and having enough to cover your expenses, save, and minimize or eliminate debt.

Financially savvy teens know that investment is most certainly *not* just for adults. In fact, some of the wealthiest investors and entrepreneurs of all time insist that money smarts should start as early as possible. Billionaire Warren Buffett, for instance, believes that parents should start helping kids become money-smart in preschool!

I hope that by this stage in your reading, you are feeling more empowered to start making decisions and taking action to ensure that your financial future is bright. Imagine buying the home of your dreams, traveling the world, and never having to worry about your and your family's expenses. You have already seen how your mastery over money starts with simple yet powerful skills such as budgeting, saving, understanding how credit works, and being ready for emergencies. And there are so many more skills to pick up as you navigate the second half of this book. If you are already seeing how important your role is in being money-smart, then I hope you can share your opinion with other teen readers.

By leaving a review of this book on Amazon, you'll help other teens see how easy it is to take the reins of their financial well-being. You can show them how easy it is to start earning, saving, and investing money right now.

By sharing your opinion about how this book has enlightened you, or pointed you in the direction of success, you can help pull other teens out of the financial literacy gap. And best of all, you only gain by sharing knowledge with others!

Thank you for your support. All teens deserve to have money management tools in their hands, and I'm so thankful that you're here to make it happen.

Scan the QR code below

BONUS BUDGETING WORKSHEETS!

As a thank you for purchasing this book, I created this worksheet for you to print whenever needed.

Scan the QR code above

Best Wishes!
Nicole Reap

CHAPTER FIVE

INVESTING AND EARNING FOR THE FUTURE

Have you ever considered how confident people make money while sleeping? Or how your saved-up pocket money can magically become a big stack of cash over the years? Let's dive into the remarkable ways you can make your cash hustle for you.

UNDERSTANDING INVESTING

Imagine being like Dylan Jin-Ngo, a 17-year-old who got hooked on the stock market in sixth grade. Now, he's not only investing but also teaching others about it. He became the youngest certified mutual fund counselor in the US in 2020, learning independently and through his non-profit, Young Investors Corp (Ferré, 2021).

Investing means you place your money in stocks or bonds, anticipating it will grow in value over time. It's a smart move for building wealth and hitting big goals, whether it's a dream home or a comfy retirement. Are you starting as a teen? That's even better. You get more time to grow your wealth thanks to compound interest. Furthermore, you acquire financial skills at an early age.

You might wonder, "What can I invest in as a teen?" You can find high-yield savings accounts, certificates of deposit (CDs), stocks, bonds, and pooled investments such as mutual funds available. A popular way to start is with a custodial account or, if you're working, a custodial IRA.

But it's not just about jumping in. Advait Arya, a high school student, started trading with about $2,180 and grew it to nearly $8,200 in a year (Nair, 2021). He used platforms like eToro, learned from online resources like Investopedia, and chose stable investments in companies like Amazon and Apple. The key? Start with a demo account to learn without risk, do your homework on companies, and avoid mindlessly following trends.

Understanding the risks and beginning the learning process early is essential. Most trading apps require you to be age 18 or older, but custodial accounts allow you to begin younger with parental supervision. This is important because it helps you learn about risk management and investment strategies in a safe environment.

Remember, investing as a teen isn't just about making money; it's about learning financial independence and responsibility. Whether inspired by stories like Dylan's or Advait's, the key is to start early, learn constantly, and invest wisely.

Different Types of Investments Suitable for Teens

You might be surprised to learn that while three-quarters of teens think investing is essential, less than a quarter have started doing it. Moreover, about half of teens feel confident about financial matters like saving and investing, which is fantastic! (*Fidelity Study*, 2023) But there's still a bit of confusion on how to get started, with many believing they're too young or unsure where to begin.

Now, onto the exciting part—investment options! First up, stocks. They're pretty neat because they often have higher returns than other investments. You can buy them in various accounts, and they're pretty relatable. Picture yourself holding a small share in a company you adore!

Next, mutual funds. These are like big pots of money, pooled from many investors and used to buy many stocks or bonds. Investing in a mutual fund means getting a slice of an extensive, diverse portfolio.

ETFs (Exchange-Traded Funds) resemble mutual funds but have recently gained more popularity. Like mutual funds, they contain a blend of stocks, bonds, or other assets, but the stock market actively trades them just like individual stocks.

Bonds stand out in their lower risk profile, typically resulting in comparatively modest returns. You lend funds to a government or company when you purchase a bond. In exchange, they commit to repaying you the borrowed amount and interest.

High-yield savings accounts provide safety and offer better interest rates than traditional ones. Their insurance covers deposits of up to $250,000, making it a highly secure method for safeguarding your money (*Deposit Insurance*, 2022).

Lastly, Certificates of Deposit (CDs) are almost risk-free and insured. But they're more of a long-term thing. You loan your money to a bank for a specific duration and receive a greater interest rate.

So, start exploring these options. Chat with your family or look up fantastic financial services companies for more information.

Always remember that the goal is to have your money actively working to benefit you, not vice versa!

THE MAGIC OF COMPOUND INTEREST

Let's discuss the concept of compound interest in a way that's straightforward to grasp. Imagine compound interest as a snowball effect on your money. It's about accumulating interest on your initial amount (your principal) and the interest already added to your principal. This distinguishes it from simple interest, where you solely receive interest based on the initial amount.

Here's an illustration to show how it operates. Suppose you save $1,000 in a bank account that offers 10% yearly compound interest. In the first year, you earn 10% of $1,000, which is $100, so now you have $1,100. In the second year, you earn 10% on this new amount ($1,100), which adds another $110 to your account, making it $1,210. This process repeats yearly, and the interest amount grows because it's calculated based on the growing account balance.

In contrast, with simple interest, if you have the same $1,000 at a 10% yearly rate, you would get $100 yearly, but only on the initial $1,000. So, after ten years, you'd have $2,000 (your original $1,000 plus $1,000 in interest). However, when it comes to compound interest, you'll see significant growth after ten years because the interest earned in each year gets added to your initial amount, and the interest for the next year is calculated based on this larger total.

Compounding can work for you in savings and investment accounts, like a 401(k) or a Roth IRA, where your money grows over time, especially if you reinvest dividends regularly. However, it can also work against you in loans and debts, like student loans or mortgages, where the interest compounds on the borrowed amount.

To maximize the power of compound interest, kickstart your savings and investments today. The longer your cash has to grow, the bigger your financial snowball will become. Also, focusing on accounts that compound interest more frequently (like daily rather than annually) can result in greater returns over time.

Understanding and utilizing compound interest's power is an intelligent way for teenagers to build wealth early. When used wisely, this tool can significantly enhance your long-term savings.

How Compound Interest Works Even on Small, Regular Investments

Imagine you start with a small amount of money, like $100, and decide to invest it wisely. Over time, your money can grow significantly, thanks to the magic of compound interest. Here's how it works:

- **Initial investment:** You start by putting your $100 into an investment account. This is your principal amount.
- **Interest earnings:** Imagine you put $100 into an account with a yearly interest rate of 5%. In the initial year, you'd gain $5 in interest (5% of $100). This boosts your total to $105.
- **Compound interest:** Here's where the magic happens. In the second year, you don't just earn 5% interest on your initial $100; you also earn it on the entire amount, which now includes the $5 interest you made in the first year. So, you earn $5.25 (5% of $105). Your total becomes $110.25.
- **Snowball effect:** Year by year, this cycle persists. As your total sum increases, so does the interest you accumulate. Each year, your capital multiplies at an accelerating pace.

- **Patience is key:** Initially, it may seem like the growth is slow, but over the long term, your money starts to grow at a much faster rate. This is why an early start is crucial.

For example, a teenager who starts investing $100 a month at age 15 and continues until age 65 could potentially have over $1 million in savings (depending on the rate of return). This shows the incredible power of compounding.

Remember, even negligible, regular investments can lead to significant wealth over time. It's about being patient, staying consistent, and letting compound interest work magic for you. So, start investing, even if it's just a tiny amount—your future self will thank you!

EARNING OPPORTUNITIES FOR TEENS

Are you a teenager aiming to earn some extra cash? Whether you're saving up for the latest gadget or starting to build your savings, there are numerous ways for teens to make money. Here's a rundown of the best side hustles and part-time jobs tailored just for you:

- **Babysitting:** It's a classic option. Many parents are looking for reliable babysitters, and you can earn a decent hourly rate.
- **Lawn care:** Offer lawn mowing and yard maintenance services in your neighborhood, especially during summer. It can be profitable.
- **Car washing:** A simple yet effective way to make money is by washing cars for friends, family, and neighbors.
- **Restaurant or retail jobs:** If you're old enough, consider working part-time in a restaurant or retail store. This

gives you a paycheck and provides worthwhile work experience.

- **Blogging:** If you're passionate about writing, consider launching a blog. You can earn income by featuring ads and engaging in affiliate marketing.
- **Programming:** Learning programming languages and offering your coding skills can be lucrative if you're tech-savvy.
- **Social media management:** Local businesses often require help managing their social media accounts, and if you excel in this area, consider offering them your social media management services.

It's essential to be aware that federal rules for working minors differ based on age and the type of job (agricultural or non-agricultural). Ensure you ascertain the rules and regulations in your locality.

Earning money as a teenager involves more than just acquiring cash. It's an opportunity to develop crucial life skills like work ethic, communication, time management, and money management. You'll also learn how to open a bank account, file taxes, and save for retirement.

The Value of Earning Your Own Money and the Sense of Independence It Brings

Earning your own money as a teenager has many benefits beyond having extra cash in your pocket. Here are some key advantages:

- **Financial independence:** When you earn your own money, you gain a sense of economic independence. You're not dependent solely on your parents or guardians to cover all your expenses. Whether buying a new gadget or saving up for a trip, you can manage your finances.

- **Responsibility:** Having a job teaches you responsibility. You learn to show up on time, complete tasks, and meet commitments. These skills are valuable in professional settings and everyday life.
- **Learning the value of money:** When you work hard for your money, you understand its value. You become more conscious of how you spend it and may even learn to budget and save for the future.
- **Saving money:** Earning your own money allows you to save for future goals, whether for college, a car, or your place. Building a financial base for the future is an excellent approach.
- **Learning to negotiate and work with people:** Jobs often involve interactions with colleagues, customers, or clients. This helps you develop critical interpersonal skills like negotiation, communication, and teamwork.
- **Sense of achievement:** It feels gratifying to earn your own hard-earned money. Each paycheck shows your effort and determination, boosting your self-esteem.
- **Creating friendships:** Workspaces provide social settings where you can forge new friendships and build connections, bringing personal and professional benefits.

For example, imagine you're working part-time at a local store. You earn money from your shifts, which allows you to buy the latest video game you've been eyeing. You also learn how to interact with customers and negotiate with suppliers, valuable skills that will serve you well in the future.

Working part-time empowers teenagers with financial freedom while fostering crucial life skills that enhance their personal and career development. Many successful individuals started their journeys by earning money as teenagers.

NOTE: You can check job apps from Money Prodigy.

URL: https://www.moneyprodigy.com/job-apps-for-teens/

As a teenager, earning money paves the way for financial independence, accountability, and personal development. It's an opportunity to learn about money, save for the future, and build valuable relationships. So, don't hesitate to explore job opportunities and start making your money work for you!

REAL STORIES OF TEEN INVESTORS AND ENTREPRENEURS

Dive into the inspiring world of teen investors and entrepreneurs, where young minds like yours are making waves. These real stories will show you how determination and creativity can turn big dreams into reality. Ready to be amazed and motivated?

Adam Hildreth: A Teenage Entrepreneur's Success Story

Adam Hildreth's journey is truly inspiring. At 14, he embarked on an entrepreneurial adventure with six friends, launching Dubit Limited, a social networking site for teenagers. Achieving this was a significant accomplishment, proving that pursuing your dreams should never be limited by your age.

By the time Adam was just 19 years old, Dubit Limited had become one of the most popular websites in the UK among teenagers. This achievement alone is a testament to what determination, creativity, and hard work can accomplish.

But Adam didn't stop there. He founded Crisp Thinking, which provides online child protection services to companies worldwide.

His dedication to making the internet a safer place for children is admirable and shows the positive impact young entrepreneurs can have on society.

Tips From Adam Hildreth's Story

- **Start early:** Don't wait for the "right" age to pursue your ideas. Adam's success story began when he was just 14.
- **Teamwork:** Collaborate with friends or like-minded individuals who share your passion and vision. Adam started his journey with six friends.
- **Innovation:** Dubit Limited started with a unique focus on meeting the specific needs of teenagers, promoting innovation and thinking outside traditional boundaries.
- **Perseverance:** There's no overnight success. Adam's journey took years of commitment and hard work.
- **Making a difference:** Consider how your ventures can positively impact society, as Adam did with Crisp Thinking.

Remember, you are never too young to achieve your goals and dreams. Adam Hildreth's journey illustrates what one can accomplish through determination and a well-defined vision.

Cory Nieves: Turning Cookies Into a Business at Age Six

Cory Nieves didn't wait until he was an adult to start his business. He embarked on his entrepreneurial adventure at just six years old! Why? It was to assist his mom in purchasing a car after their move from the Bronx to Englewood, New Jersey.

Imagine being a young kid, already contemplating improving your family's life. That's precisely what Cory did. He identified an opportunity and took decisive action.

He started selling cookies in his hometown, and his business quickly became popular. People loved his cookies, and word spread like wildfire. Today, Mr. Cory's Cookies sells thousands of cookies every week!

Cory's Story Teaches Us Some Valuable Lessons:

- **Start small, dream big:** Cory had a small plan when he started—he just wanted to help his mom. But his small venture turned into something huge. This shows that you don't need to have everything figured out from the start.
- **Perseverance pays off:** When faced with challenges such as health code violations leading to the closure of his cookie business, Cory persevered. He continued to put in effort and discovered ways to overcome these obstacles.
- **Quality matters:** Mr. Cory's Cookies became successful not just because of Cory's determination but also because he offered a quality product. Always aim for greatness in your endeavors.
- **Community support:** Cory's success wasn't just about him; his family played a crucial role in supporting his dreams. Have people who have faith in your aspirations in your circle.

Cory Nieves demonstrates that entrepreneurship is not bound by age, proving that you can start a business at any age. So, if you've got a business idea or a dream, don't let your age hold you back. Start small, work hard. You might be the next teen entrepreneur making waves!

Remember that plenty of teenagers have left their mark as successful young entrepreneurs—you're not alone in your journey. With perseverance and the right attitude, you can attain your objectives just like Cory did.

Continue to dream, put in the effort, and believe in yourself! Your entrepreneurial journey may become the next incredible success story we encounter.

COMPOUND INTEREST WORKSHEET

Before we start with the scenarios, it's crucial to understand the compound interest formula. Here it is:

$$A = P(1 + \tfrac{r}{n})^{nt}$$

Where:

- A is the amount of money accumulated after n years, including interest.
- P is the principal amount (the initial sum of money).
- r is the annual interest rate (decimal).
- n represents how frequently interest compounds within a year.
- t is the time the money stays in an investment, measured in years.

Let's move on to real-life scenarios to see how this works in action!

Scenario 1: Saving for a Dream Vacation

Imagine you've saved $5,000 to put towards a dream vacation. You find a savings account that offers a 4% annual interest rate, compounded quarterly. You plan to go on your vacation in 5 years. How much money will you have saved by that time?

Solution:

- Principal (P) = $5,000
- Annual interest rate (r) = 4% or 0.04 (as a decimal)
- Number of times compounded annually (n) = 4 (quarterly)
- Time (t) = 5 years

Using the formula:

$A = 5000(1 + \frac{0.04}{4})^{4 \times 5}$

$A = 5000(1 + 0.01)^{20}$
$A = 5000(1.01)^{20}$
$A = 5000 \times 1.219$
$A = \$6,095$

So, in 5 years, you'll have $6,095 for your vacation. That's an extra $1,095 earned just by letting your money grow!

Scenario 2: College Fund for Your Child

Your parents started a college fund with $10,000 when you were a child, with an interest rate of 3% compounded annually. How much will be in the fund when your child turns 18?

Scenario 3: Retirement Savings

You're 30 and start with $20,000 in your retirement fund. The fund has an annual return of 5%, compounded monthly. What will the value be when you retire at 65?

Scenario 4: Buying a Car

You put $2,000 in a high-yield savings account to buy a new car. The account offers a 2.5% interest rate, compounded monthly. What will your total be in three years?

Scenario 5: Growing Your Emergency Fund

You have an emergency fund of $3,000. You find an account offering a 3.5% annual interest rate, compounded semi-annually. How much will this fund grow to in 10 years?

In each scenario, the magic of compound interest works in your favor. Understanding how the formula works and being patient can see your savings grow significantly over time. Remember that the crucial thing is to begin early and allow time to impact your investments positively!

KEY TAKEAWAYS

- Compound interest is a powerful financial tool that allows your savings and investments to grow over time by earning interest on both the principal and accumulated interest.
- Teens have various investment options, including stocks, mutual funds, ETFs, bonds, high-yield savings accounts, and CDs, each with unique benefits and risks.
- Understanding and utilizing compound interest from a young age can significantly boost long-term savings and wealth accumulation.
- Making consistent and modest investments can significantly increase in value thanks to the compounding effect, like a snowball rolling downhill and getting bigger.

- There are numerous earning opportunities for teens, including classic options like babysitting and lawn care as well as modern ones like blogging and social media management.
- Earning your own money as a teenager brings financial independence, responsibility, life skills, savings opportunities, and a sense of achievement.
- The compound interest formula is vital to understanding how investments grow, and real-life scenarios illustrate its practical application in savings for goals like vacations, college funds, retirement, and emergency funds.
- Starting early with investments and understanding compound interest is crucial for long-term financial growth and success.

You're on the right track! Take action on these ideas to boost your financial game. Next up, get ready to explore entrepreneurship and digital finance tools in the next chapter. It's all about taking your financial journey to the next level!

CHAPTER SIX

ENTREPRENEURSHIP AND NAVIGATING DIGITAL FINANCE

Did you realize that many top entrepreneurs kickstarted their first ventures as teens? In today's digital era, handling money and launching a business is easier than ever. Let's delve into how you can begin by nurturing an entrepreneurial mindset.

CULTIVATING AN ENTREPRENEURIAL MINDSET

Thinking like an entrepreneur isn't just about starting a business; it's a mindset that can benefit you in many aspects of life, from school to your future career. Imagine having the determination to face challenges head-on, the focus to stay on track amidst distractions, and the drive to turn your ideas into reality. These are traits that successful entrepreneurs embody, and they're traits you can develop, too, regardless of whether you're planning to start your own business.

Let's break it down:

- **Determination:** Entrepreneurs don't let failure stop them. They view challenges as chances to expand their knowledge and evolve. For example, consider a time when you struggled with a complex math problem. Instead of giving up, you persisted until you found a solution. That's determination in action.

- **Focus:** Entrepreneurs know how to prioritize and avoid getting sidetracked. For example, when you have a big project due at school, you must stay focused to finish it on time despite other distractions like social media or video games.

- **Drive:** Entrepreneurs are driven by their passion for ideas, dedicating themselves to hard work to bring them to life. This zeal fuels the development of positive habits and ensures they remain focused on achieving their objectives. Maybe you have a hobby or interest you're passionate about, like playing an instrument or coding. That same drive can also help you excel in other areas of your life.

- **Decisiveness:** Entrepreneurs must make quick decisions to keep their businesses running smoothly. Similarly, in your life, being able to make decisions efficiently can save you time and energy. Whether choosing what to study in college or picking a career path, being decisive is a valuable skill.

- **Independence:** Entrepreneurs boldly take control and chase their ambitions, even when it means challenging the status quo. Maybe you've seen someone at school start a club or project on their initiative. That's the spirit of independence in action.

- **Authenticity:** Entrepreneurs are genuine and passionate about their ideas, even when others doubt them. This authenticity helps them build trust and credibility with others. Remaining faithful to your convictions and values can earn you respect and support among your friends.

- **Flexibility:** Entrepreneurs are always ready to adapt and change course when needed. In today's ever-changing world, adaptability is essential to keep up with the rapid pace of evolution. For example, maybe you've had to adjust your study schedule to accommodate changes in your extracurricular activities or family responsibilities.
- **A thirst for knowledge:** Entrepreneurs continuously strive to learn and enhance their skills, embodying the spirit of lifelong learning. By pursuing education and embracing new experiences, you, too, can unlock opportunities and achieve your ambitions.
- **Creativity:** Entrepreneurs excel at thinking creatively, crafting novel solutions and innovative products, or applying unique perspectives to conventional tasks like a school project. This inventive approach is crucial, no matter the challenge or the realm of work.

So, even if you're not planning to start your own business, embracing the entrepreneurial mindset can help you succeed in school, your future career, and life. It's all about being determined, focused, and driven to pursue your passions and turn your ideas into reality.

FIRST STEPS IN ENTREPRENEURSHIP

Starting your small venture can be both exciting and daunting, but don't worry, we've got you covered with some essential steps to get you started on the right track:

- **Think of your Business Idea:** Begin by brainstorming what you're passionate about or what problems you see around you that you could solve. Whether creating handmade crafts, offering tutoring services, or starting a pet-sitting business, choose something you love and believe in.

- **Create a business plan:** Once you've settled on your idea, it's crucial to record it. Detail your objectives, identify your target audience, devise your pricing approach, and determine your funding strategy. A robust business plan maintains your focus and can draw in potential investors if required.

- **Choose a structure and register your business:** Choose the legal form for your company, such as a sole proprietorship, partnership, or LLC. Afterward, register your business name and acquire the necessary licenses or permits to function within the law.

- **Set up your business operations:** This includes everything from finding a location (if necessary) to setting up your online presence through a website or social media accounts. Ensure you possess the essential tools and resources to provide your products or services efficiently.

- **Understand your rules, regulations, and taxes:** Familiarize yourself with the laws and regulations that apply to your business, such as health and safety standards or zoning laws. Also, learn about your tax obligations as a business owner to avoid surprises come tax time.

- **Learn how to maintain your teen business:** Operating a business involves ongoing education. Keep receptive to feedback, adjust to market changes, and actively search for chances to grow and enhance.

- **Don't stop learning from others:** Connect with fellow entrepreneurs, join online forums or local business groups, and seek mentorship from experienced professionals. Acquiring wisdom from the ventures of others can offer practical lessons and prevent you from encountering typical mistakes.

Launching a business demands commitment, persistence, and patience. Maintain your focus on your objectives, and don't hesitate to pursue help when necessary. Your small venture can flourish and become a rewarding entrepreneurship journey with the right mindset and preparation.

Practical Strategies to Start and Grow Your Business Ideas

Launching and expanding your business as a teenager may feel overwhelming, but you can transform your visions into tangible achievements with effective strategies. Here are some simple yet effective tips to kickstart your entrepreneurial journey:

- **Streaming:** Dive into content creation by streaming your gaming sessions, sharing your expertise on a particular topic, or showcasing your creativity through art or music. You can leverage Twitch, YouTube, and TikTok platforms to connect with a broad audience and earn money from your content through advertisements, sponsorships, and donations.
- **E-commerce:** Tap into the booming online marketplace by starting your e-commerce store. Whether you're selling handmade crafts, custom merchandise, or trendy fashion items, platforms like Shopify, Etsy, and eBay provide easy-to-use tools to set up and manage your online storefront.
- **When mom gives you lemons, make lemonade:** Seize the unexpected opportunities that arise. If your mom offers you lemons from the backyard, turn them into a refreshing

lemonade stand business. This simple yet classic example teaches you to be resourceful and maximize what you have.

- **Get crafty:** Put your creativity to work by making one-of-a-kind products tailored for specific niche markets. Whether hand-painted sneakers, custom jewelry, or personalized phone cases, your artistic skills can translate into profitable ventures, especially on platforms like Etsy and Instagram.
- **Design websites and online stores:** Utilize your web design and coding skills by providing services to small businesses or individuals aiming to establish an online presence. People will likely seek your expertise as the demand for appealing, user-friendly websites increases.
- **Use your "social" skills:** Leverage your social media presence to promote your products or services and engage with potential customers. Establish a solid personal brand and nurture connections with your audience to boost traffic and increase sales for your business.
- **Dip your toe into AI:** Delve into the captivating realm of artificial intelligence by incorporating AI-powered solutions into your business processes. Whether using chatbots for customer support, implementing predictive analytics for sales forecasting, or leveraging machine learning algorithms for personalized recommendations, AI can enhance efficiency and innovation in your ventures.

Remember that entrepreneurship entails facing challenges and rewards along the journey. Stay curious, persistent, and adaptable, and you'll be well on your way to turning your business dreams into reality.

NAVIGATING DIGITAL FINANCE

Today, managing personal and business finances has become easier than ever thanks to the convenience offered by digital tools in our rapidly evolving world. From online banking to budgeting apps and digital payment systems, these tools are crucial in helping you stay on top of your financial game. Let's dive into how these digital marvels make your life simpler and more organized.

Create Engaging and Interactive Experiences

Say goodbye to the old days of boring manual math and paperwork. With digital tools, managing your finances becomes an engaging and interactive experience. Picture this: you're using a budgeting app that breaks down your expenses into colorful charts and graphs, helping you visualize where your money goes each month. It's like a game where you strive to beat your high score in saving money!

Immediate Feedback

One of the perks of digital tools is the instant feedback they provide. Whether checking your account balance or reviewing your spending habits, you get immediate insights into your financial status. Imagine swiping through your banking app and seeing a notification alerting you to an upcoming bill payment. It's akin to always having a financial advisor with you, ensuring you're constantly informed.

Accessibility

With digital tools, your finances are just a few taps away, 24/7. You can easily access your accounts, whether relaxing on the couch or waiting for your next class to begin. Say goodbye to long lines at the bank or waiting for paper statements to arrive in the mail. Everything you need is right at your fingertips, ready whenever you are.

Personalization

Every financial journey is unique, and digital tools understand that. These apps customize their features to match your individual needs and objectives. For example, certain budgeting apps enable you to establish personalized spending categories that align with your lifestyle. Whether you're a music lover splurging on concert tickets or a foodie indulging in gourmet meals, the app adapts to your preferences, helping you stay on track without sacrificing your passions.

Now, let's explore some practical features offered by these digital tools:

- **Check balances on accounts and view records of your transactions:** Imagine being able to glance at your phone and see exactly how much money you have in your checking account, along with a detailed list of your recent transactions. It's like having a virtual piggy bank that never runs out of coins!
- **Set up auto payments effortlessly:** Ensure you never miss bill deadlines or incur late fees again. With auto payment options, you can set up recurring payments for your bills and relax knowing that everything is taken care of automatically. It's financial freedom at its finest!
- **Transfer funds between accounts:** Transferring funds from your savings to your checking account is a breeze! With just a few clicks, you can seamlessly move money

between accounts, guaranteeing you always have the required cash.

- **Save or print statements for your tax or personal records:** Tax season doesn't have to be stressful. Digital tools make it easy to download or print statements for your tax or personal records, simplifying the process of filing your taxes and keeping track of your financial history.

As merchants and consumers embrace e-commerce and digital shopping habits, the adoption of digital payment methods continues to soar. A recent Statista study forecasts that by 2028, digital payments will surge worldwide to $16.62 trillion (*Digital Payments*, n.d.). The movement towards electronic and contactless payments results from their convenience, enhanced security, and the rising trend of shopping online.

Thanks to digital tools, we're witnessing a revolution in managing personal and business finances. From online banking to budgeting apps and digital payment systems, these tools offer engaging experiences, immediate feedback, accessibility, and personalization. So why wait? Take control of your finances today and embrace the power of digital tools to secure your financial future.

MONEY MANAGEMENT APPS YOU CAN USE TO TAKE CHARGE OF YOUR FINANCES

Mastering money management as a teen is vital for your future finances. Whether aiming for a new gadget or preparing for college costs, early adoption of financial skills is critical. That's why we've curated a selection of tailored money management apps to empower you to take charge of your finances.

Banking and Money Management Apps

These apps serve as your go-to tools for general banking and money management. They offer many features to help you handle your finances efficiently.

- **FamZoo:** FamZoo simplifies managing your allowance and expenses by linking your parent's accounts with yours. With features like debit cards and budgeting tools, it's an excellent option for teens looking to make the most of their money.
- **BusyKid:** Earn cash with BusyKid by completing chores and tasks your parents assign. This app helps you manage your earnings and teaches responsibility and accountability.
- **Axos First Checking:** Experience the freedom of traditional banking with Axos First Checking. From debit cards to savings accounts, it provides everything you need to kickstart your financial journey.

Budgeting and Saving Apps

These apps aim to assist you in setting aside funds for your specific goals and crafting detailed budgets to meet your financial needs.

- **Current:** Current offers a range of features, including budgeting tools and direct deposit. Its reduced fees make it an attractive option for teens looking to manage their money effectively.
- **YNAB:** You Need a Budget (YNAB) provides comprehensive budgeting resources to help you learn and practice practical money management skills. With classes

and online videos, it's more than just an app—it's a valuable financial education tool.

- **Toshl Finance:** Analyze your spending habits and track your finances with Toshl Finance. Its user-friendly interface and "Left-to-Spend" feature make it ideal for teens looking to understand their spending patterns.

Investing Apps

Even with limited funds, investing apps allow you to dip your toes into investing and grow your money over time.

- **Acorns:** Start investing with as little as $3 using Acorns. With features like save-to-invest and cashback rewards, it's a beginner-friendly option for teens interested in building wealth.
- **Stash:** Stash offers a variety of beginner investment options and budgeting tools to help you diversify your money. While it requires some financial knowledge, it's an excellent platform for learning about investing.

Money-Saving Apps

These apps help you save money on everyday purchases and manage your subscriptions more efficiently.

- **SplashMoney:** Import all your accounts into SplashMoney for easy access and management. Its spending reports provide valuable insights into your financial habits.
- **Rocket Money.** Rocket Money helps you track and manage your subscriptions, ensuring you don't overspend on unnecessary services. It's a valuable tool for teens looking to save money and stay financially organized.

Money-Making Apps

Explore non-traditional ways to earn money with these apps, whether through surveys, shopping rewards, or reviewing phone calls.

- **Swagbucks:** Earn rewards by shopping, taking surveys, and more with Swagbucks. It offers flexible earning options and cashouts via PayPal or gift cards.
- **Humanatic:** Get paid to review recorded phone calls with Humanatic. It's a unique opportunity to earn money while gaining valuable experience in quality assurance.

Debt Apps

Learn how to manage debt effectively with these apps, which offer tools and resources to help you stay on top of your financial obligations.

- **GoHenry:** Manage your debit card and learn debt management techniques with GoHenry. Its video lessons and quizzes make understanding and applying financial concepts easy.
- **Tally:** Consolidate your debt into one monthly payment with Tally. While geared towards older teens, it helps simplify debt management and lower interest payments.

Mastering financial management during your teenage years is an invaluable skill that will significantly benefit you in the long run. With these money management apps, you can build a strong foundation for your financial future today.

STORIES OF TEEN ENTREPRENEURS

Dive into the world of teenage entrepreneurs like Jack Bonneau, Riya Karumanchi, and Maya Penn who show us that age is just a number for innovation. From lemonade stands to intelligent canes and sustainable fashion, their stories inspire action. Let's explore how they turned their dreams into realities, proving that you can make a significant impact with creativity, tech-savviness, and determination.

Jack Bonneau: Teen Hustle

Meet Jack Bonneau, 13, the brains behind Jack's Stands & Marketplaces. At 8, he craved a $400 LEGO set, so he launched a lemonade stand, raking in $900 in 12 weeks. Now, he helps kids set up their stands for $15, teaching them business basics. Transitioning Jack's Stands into a nonprofit, he plans to expand nationwide. His latest venture, Teen Hustl, aims to connect tech-savvy teens with gig economy jobs, like hyper-local delivery services. Jack's inspiring journey proves teens can turn their passions into successful ventures with creativity and determination.

Riya Karumanchi: SmartCane

Imagine being just 14 and inventing the SmartCane, a game-changing upgrade to the traditional white cane used by blind individuals. Riya Karumanchi's encounter with her friend's visually impaired grandmother sparked the idea. Motivated by the shortcomings of conventional canes, she felt compelled to enhance the quality of life for people with visual impairments. With $56,000 in initial funding from investors like Microsoft, Riya founded SmartCane at Ryerson University. As CEO, she's transformed the lives of 285 million visually impaired individuals and earned 16 awards. Riya's innovation proves that age is no barrier to profoundly impacting the world.

Maya Penn: Maya's Ideas

Maya Penn's mom encouraged Maya, at just eight years old, to pursue her dream of sustainable fashion. Learning HTML at 10, she launched Maya's Ideas, employing ten and selling globally. Her first sale thrilled her, driving her passion for creation. Now 19, Maya also founded Maya's Ideas 4 the Planet, advocating eco-friendly products for women. Animated shorts presented to Congress and three TED Talks later, she's earned millions, securing $500,000 from investors. Despite her success, Maya stresses self-care, advocating walks and reading to stay grounded. Remember, self-care enhances your entrepreneurial journey.

These inspiring teens like Jack Bonneau, Riya Karumanchi, and Maya Penn utilized digital tools to fuel their success. From launching lemonade stands to inventing life-changing devices, they leveraged technology at every step. Jack used online resources to teach business basics and expand his lemonade empire. Riya utilized digital platforms for funding and networking, transforming her SmartCane vision into reality. Maya utilized digital marketing and e-commerce to grow Maya's Ideas globally. Their stories show that you can also realize your dreams with digital tools, determination, and creativity.

MY FIRST BUSINESS PLAN TEMPLATE

Crafting a business plan might seem monumental, but it's your first step toward realizing your dreams. Think of it as mapping your path to success, starting with a clear idea and understanding of where you want to go. Here's a no-frills template to kickstart your venture as an entrepreneur:

- **Executive summary:** Kick things off with a bang! Summarize your business, the problem it solves, and why it will be a hit. Imagine telling your best friend about your excellent business idea, but you only have a minute to get them as excited about it as you are.
- **Business description:** Explore the business idea further in this area. What exactly is your business? What makes it unique? This is where you share your vision, the core of your business, and how it stands out from the crowd.
- **Products and services:** What are you selling or offering? Describe your products or services in detail. If you plan to sell handmade jewelry, what makes your pieces different from what's already out there? Think about the special touch you bring to the table.
- **Market analysis:** Who are you selling to? Specify your target audience and explain why they need your product or service. It's like choosing who to invite to your party because you know they'll love it.
- **Strategy and implementation:** How will you reach your customers? Describe how you will advertise your business and promote your products or services to attract customers. Whether through Instagram, word-of-mouth, or flyers at school, have a plan to get people talking.
- **Organizational structure:** Who's in charge of what? If it's just you, that's cool, but if you're teaming up with friends, lay out who does what. Creating a band is similar; each member must understand their role.
- **Financial plan and projections:** What initial investment is required and what are your revenue streams? Even if it's just an approximation, having a financial plan

demonstrates your commitment to making this venture successful.

Remember, this plan is for you. It doesn't have to be perfect, but it should guide you towards making your business a reality. Think of it as a flexible document that grows with your business, adapting to its development and changes. The most important part is to start. As you learn and your business expands, so will your plan.

You can find some of the best templates at Kid's Money if you want a business plan.

URL: https://www.kidsmoney.org/teens/earning/entrepreneur ship/business-plans/

KEY TAKEAWAYS

- An entrepreneurial mindset, focusing on traits like determination, focus, drive, decisiveness, independence, authenticity, flexibility, a thirst for knowledge, and creativity, benefits all aspects of life.
- Starting a business involves brainstorming ideas, creating a business plan, choosing a legal structure, setting up operations, understanding regulations and taxes, and continuous learning and adaptation.
- Digital finance tools, including online banking, budgeting apps, and digital payments, simplify managing personal and business finances, offering immediate feedback, accessibility, and personalized experiences.
- A basic business plan outline for teenagers comprises an executive summary, a description of the business, details on products and services, market analysis, strategy for

implementation, organizational structure, and financial projections.

Now's the time to turn those entrepreneurial dreams into reality! Dive into the insights and digital strategies this chapter shares and start your journey toward financial independence. Next, we'll explore intelligent financial strategies to build wealth and sustain independence, arming you with the tools you need for a secure financial future. Get ready to make your mark!

CHAPTER SEVEN

PATHWAY TO WEALTH AND INDEPENDENCE

Surprisingly, grasping the difference between assets and liabilities isn't just for grown-ups. It's your ticket to getting ahead. Think of it as knowing what's filling your piggy bank versus what's sneaking money out. Ready to dive in? Let's unlock this financial mystery together and set you up for success.

ASSETS VS. LIABILITIES

Diving into the world of finances might be off your daily to-do list, but understanding the basics of assets and liabilities can seriously amp up your game for the future. Let's simplify it so it's relevant to you.

Assets represent valuable possessions that you own and can convert into cash. Think about the stuff in your life: your smartphone, your gaming console, even the money you've stashed away from birthday gifts or part-time jobs. These are all assets because they're worth something and can put cash in your pocket. And it's not just about the tangible stuff you can touch; intangible things count, too. If you've ever created an app or written a piece of music, the copyrights or patents on those creations are also assets.

On the flip side, liabilities represent your obligations to others. This could be as simple as the money you promised to pay back to a friend who paid for your movie ticket. It might look like student loans or a car loan. Even though you might not be dealing with a mortgage right now, it's a standard liability for many adults, where the house is an asset, but the amount still owed on it is the liability.

It's essential to grasp the significant distinctions between assets and liabilities. It boils down to their nature (what you own vs. what you owe), ownership (assets are yours, liabilities are claims others have on you), and financial impact (assets can boost your wealth, liabilities can reduce it).

So, how do assets contribute to wealth while liabilities detract from it? Imagine your assets are like seeds you plant in a garden. Over time, with the proper care, those seeds grow and multiply, increasing your garden's overall value. That's precisely how assets like savings accounts, investments, or even valuable skills can expand your wealth over time. Liabilities, though, are like weeds. They can choke out your garden's growth if you're careless, draining your resources and leaving you with less.

Effective management of your assets and liabilities is critical to building that wealth. Consider investing in yourself and your future as part of your asset-building strategy. This could mean saving part of your allowance or job earnings, investing in stocks or bonds, or acquiring new skills that could pay off. For liabilities, the goal is to keep them under control. This means being smart about borrowing (like not racking up unnecessary debt on things that don't grow in value) and planning to pay off any debts you have.

Remember, the choices you make today about managing your assets and liabilities can set the foundation for your financial future. It's not just about saving every penny or avoiding all debt; it's about making informed decisions that balance what you own with what you owe. This way, you're not just surviving your financial journey but thriving, building a wealthier and more secure future for yourself.

BUILDING ASSETS

As a teenager, the world of finance might seem daunting, but it's filled with opportunities to build assets and secure your financial future. Whether saving money, investing wisely, or starting a small business, there are plenty of practical ways to get ahead. Let's explore some relatable and actionable strategies.

First, consider doing chores and odd jobs around your house or neighborhood. This can be a simple way to earn some cash while lending a hand. Whether mowing lawns, shoveling snow, or washing cars, your efforts can translate into a tidy sum of money.

Babysitting, dog walking, and pet sitting are also great options. They not only pay well but can help you develop responsibility and trustworthiness. Plus, it's a chance to prove your reliability to your neighbors and earn more through referrals.

Selling your belongings online or in person can help tidy up your space while boosting your wallet. The second-hand market offers many items, including old video games, books, and clothes you've outgrown or no longer use.

For entrepreneurs, why not start a lemonade stand in the summer or a hot cocoa stand in the winter? It's a classic and can teach you the basics of running a business, from cost management to customer service.

Consider sharing your skills or hobbies by teaching others. Sharing knowledge can be rewarding and profitable, whether it's guitar lessons, soccer coaching, or art classes.

Online platforms offer even more opportunities. Teens can use sites like Nextdoor to find local gigs, freelance for various projects, or tutor peers in subjects they excel in. Online surveys might only pay a little, but they can be a good starting point to get used to earning your own money.

For creative and tech-savvy people, monetizing social media accounts or streaming on platforms like Twitch could be the way to go. Growing a following requires time and dedication but can lead to significant financial rewards.

Remember, these ventures provide you with an income and invaluable life skills. They teach you about work ethic, financial management, and the value of money. Plus, the satisfaction of earning your own money is unmatched.

Always stay aware of the opportunities around you, and don't be afraid to try new things. With ambition and effort, you can start building your financial assets today.

MINIMIZING LIABILITIES

Making smart financial decisions as a teenager sets the stage for a stable and thriving future. It's all about understanding where you stand financially, making informed decisions, and adopting habits that shield you from liabilities and ensure smart spending and borrowing. Now, let's explore how you can achieve that.

Know Where You Stand

Before taking any further steps, ensure you clearly understand your financial situation. This means knowing how much money you have, how much you owe (if anything), and where your money goes each month. Imagine it as taking a quick picture of your wallet. A straightforward approach is to monitor your expenses for a month. Use an app or a notebook—whatever works for you. You might be surprised to see how much those weekend outings or online purchases add up.

Set a Budget

Once you've monitored your spending, creating a budget is essential. Consider your budget as a roadmap guiding your spending decisions. It's not about limiting yourself but empowering your money to serve your goals. Allocate funds for your needs (like food and transportation), savings, and wants. Remember, a budget that's too tight is challenging to stick to, so be realistic.

Eliminate Debt

If you've borrowed money—maybe you have a credit card or a loan for a big purchase—it's crucial to pay this off as soon as possible. Interest can accumulate quickly, turning a small debt into a mountain. Try the "snowball method": start by paying off your smallest debts to build momentum, then move on to the larger ones. This reduces your debt and gives you psychological wins that keep you motivated.

Build an Emergency Fund

Life throws curveballs, and not all of them are enjoyable. An emergency fund is a financial safety cushion for unforeseen expenses, such as a cracked phone screen or an impromptu journey. Make it a goal to save enough money to cover your living expenses for three to six months. Start small if you need to; even saving a little bit each month can build a robust fund over time.

Prefund Major Purchases

Are you planning to buy something big, like a new laptop or a car? Start saving now. This "pre-funding" approach helps you avoid debt by saving up for major purchases ahead of time. It also gives you the time to shop around for the best deals and make more informed decisions.

Systematically Save and Invest

Finally, make saving and investing a habit. Even small amounts saved today can grow significantly thanks to compound interest. Consider arranging automatic savings account transfers or investing in a low-risk mutual fund. The key is consistency; it's not about how much you save and invest but how often.

Responsible management of your finances is about making wise choices now to set yourself up for a brighter future. It might seem challenging at first, but with a little effort and discipline, you can avoid liabilities, save for your dreams, and build a life of financial freedom. Remember, the best time to start is now.

STEPS TO FINANCIAL INDEPENDENCE

Embarking on the journey toward financial independence as a teenager is a commendable goal that requires discipline, knowledge, and a proactive approach. This guide outlines practical steps for reaching financial independence, stressing the significance of financial education and strategic planning:

- **Set clear financial goals:** Define your financial goals, whether saving for a car, paying for college, or creating an emergency fund. Craft SMART goals—specific, measurable, achievable, relevant, and time-bound—to guide your financial journey with clarity and purpose.
- **Budget wisely:** Creating a budget is foundational to managing your finances. Identify your income sources and fixed expenses and allocate savings and discretionary spending funds. Keeping track of where your money goes can help you make informed decisions about spending and saving.
- **Prioritize saving:** Treat saving as a non-negotiable part of your budget. Before spending on anything else, allocate some of your income to savings. Experts recommend starting with an emergency fund that covers 3-6 months of expenses, then moving on to save for specific goals (Sabatier, 2023).
- **Learn to invest:** Once you have a solid savings base, consider investing to grow your wealth over time. Explore options like the stock market, mutual funds, and bonds. Starting early and thinking long-term is vital for successful investing.
- **Earn your own money:** Gaining financial independence requires having your source of income. Part-time jobs,

freelancing, or starting a small business can provide money, valuable work experience, and skills.

- **Manage debt wisely:** Grasp the distinction between beneficial and harmful debt. While some debt, like student loans, can be considered an investment in your future, avoid high-interest debt such as credit card balances. Learning to use credit responsibly is crucial for maintaining financial health.

- **Continue your financial education:** Keep learning actively to stay on top of personal finance. Dive into books, follow trusted finance blogs, and utilize educational materials to boost your understanding and abilities. This will empower you to make smart financial decisions throughout your life.

- **Embrace technology:** Leverage financial apps and tools to manage your budget, track expenses, and invest. Many platforms offer tailored services for young investors, making it easier to navigate your financial landscape.

- **Practice financial discipline:** Developing self-discipline in spending is vital. Distinguish between desires and necessities, and practice delayed gratification to prioritize long-term financial objectives over immediate wants.

- **Plan for the future:** Teenagers should start planning for retirement as early as possible. Think about opening a retirement account such as a Roth IRA. An early start can significantly boost the growth of your savings, all thanks to compound interest.

Remember, the path to financial independence is a marathon, not a sprint. Achieving this requires patience, persistence, and a readiness to learn from errors. By taking these steps and consistently educating yourself about personal finance, you can construct a robust financial base that will benefit you throughout your adult life and beyond.

CALCULATING NET WORTH

Calculating your net worth isn't just an activity for the wealthy; it's a valuable exercise for everyone, including you. Understanding your net worth gives a clear picture of your financial health, helping you make informed spending, saving, and investing decisions. Think of it as a financial health check-up: it's essential, and the sooner you start, the better.

Net worth equals your assets minus your liabilities. To calculate it, you'll add up all your assets—anything you own that has monetary value—and then subtract all your liabilities, which are the debts or obligations that subtract from your resources. This might seem difficult, but let's simplify it with examples that relate to your life.

Assets: Your Financial Building Blocks

Assets include:

- cash in your bank accounts.
- investments (like stocks, bonds, or cryptocurrency).
- real estate (if you own your home).
- personal property with value (think of a car, a high-end laptop, or even collectible sneakers).

For a teenager, assets might be more straightforward—savings accounts, a paycheck from a part-time job, or even valuable electronics or a bicycle.

Liabilities: What You Owe

Liabilities represent your obligations to others. This includes car loans, credit card debt, student loans, or money you've committed to paying back to someone. For many teenagers, liabilities might be minimal, but they can also include things like owing money on a smartphone plan or a personal loan from a family member.

Putting It All Together: Calculating Your Net Worth

To figure out your net worth, deduct the total amount you owe from the total value of your assets. If the result is positive, that's excellent news—you've got more assets than liabilities. But if it's negative, it means your liabilities outweigh your assets. This is a crucial point: a positive net worth signals good financial health, indicating you're likely managing your finances well and have some financial security. However, a negative net worth suggests it's time to take a step back and carefully review your spending and saving habits.

Let's look at a relatable example. Imagine you have $1,000 in a savings account (asset), a laptop worth $500 (asset), and you owe $200 on a credit card (liability). Your net worth would be $1,300 (the total of your assets) minus $200 (your liability), equaling a net worth of $1,100. Not too shabby for a start!

Why Your Net Worth Matters

Knowing your net worth isn't just about tracking a number—it's about understanding your financial footing. A positive and growing net worth over time is a sign you're moving in the right direction and making intelligent financial choices. If your net worth decreases, it's a nudge to look at your spending habits, reduce unnecessary expenses, and perhaps increase your savings rate.

Younger generations are increasingly focusing on financial literacy and health. Starting early empowers you to lay the groundwork for a financially stable future. Remember, the goal isn't to obsess over every penny but to have a realistic overview of your financial situation.

Calculating your net worth is a crucial step in managing your finances. Understanding and using your financial standing to make informed decisions is critical for a better economic future. Begin tracking your net worth now; this habit will benefit you long-term. Remember, achieving financial health is a journey, not a race. Each step toward enhancing your net worth brings you closer to greater economic independence and security.

SUCCESS STORIES

Kennedy Miller's path to financial independence is an inspiring tale of early education in personal finance, careful saving, and strategic foresight. Growing up in a family that valued open discussions about money, Kennedy and their siblings were introduced to financial concepts at a young age through a home-schooling curriculum designed by their forward-thinking parents. This early exposure was crucial in developing Kennedy's financially astute mindset.

Initially overwhelmed by financial responsibilities, Kennedy's outlook transformed after engaging in personal finance education, especially a teenage-targeted book, *First to a Million*. This book highlighted the freedom financial independence could offer, motivating Kennedy to pursue a future not tied down by unsatisfying work.

Embracing the concept of compound interest, Kennedy learned to differentiate between beneficial and detrimental types of interest, choosing to capitalize on the former through intelligent savings and investments. Starting with an annual saving of $1,000 at 15 and aiming for a 7% return, Kennedy sought to build a considerable sum by 40, showcasing the advantages of starting young.

Kennedy took advantage of their youthful stage, free from significant financial burdens, to save, invest, and spend wisely under their parents' guidance. This balance allowed for enjoyment without compromising future savings goals. Moreover, Kennedy worked on establishing a solid credit history early by using their parents' credit cards responsibly, setting a foundation for a strong credit score.

Kennedy's story emphasizes the value of early financial education, the power of compound interest, and living within one's means for teenagers. By beginning their financial independence journey early, Kennedy demonstrates how young people can secure a financially stable and fulfilling retirement.

ASSET AND LIABILITY SORTING EXERCISE

Let's play a game to sharpen your understanding of assets and liabilities. It's super important to get why knowing the difference between the two can be a game changer for your financial future. Ready? Here's your mission: I will list many items, and you'll decide whether each is an asset or a liability. Remember that assets add to your funds, whereas liabilities subtract from them.

Here's your list:

- savings account
- car loan

- smartphone you own
- credit card debt
- your computer used for gaming
- mortgage on a house
- a book collection
- student loans
- investment in stocks
- bicycle for commuting to work

Think of it this way: If it's something that could earn you money or you could sell for cash, it's likely an asset. If it's something you owe money on, it's a liability. Put each item in the correct category and see how you do. This isn't just about right or wrong answers; it's about understanding why each item belongs where it does. Ready to find out how money-savvy you are?

KEY TAKEAWAYS

- Assets comprise valuable possessions or investments capable of generating income or being sold for cash.
- Liabilities represent debts or obligations that diminish your financial resources.
- Managing assets and liabilities effectively is crucial for boosting net worth.
- Compound interest, distinguishing between good and bad, significantly impacts wealth accumulation.
- Practicing frugality and smart spending without sacrificing quality of life can boost savings.
- Building a solid credit history is crucial for your future financial well-being.

- Engaging with personal finance education and practical experience from a young age can set a strong foundation for financial independence.

With a clear understanding of your assets, liabilities, and net worth, it's time to implement these concepts. Take the initial stride toward financial independence. The next chapter will explore the dynamic balance between risk and reward in your economic choices. Get set to elevate your financial skills!

CHAPTER EIGHT

RISK, REWARD, AND PLANNING FOR THE FUTURE

Do you think you're playing it safe by keeping your cash under the mattress? Guess again! Not investing might be your most significant risk. Let's dive into the world of risk and reward together so you're all set to make smart money moves for a bright financial future.

UNDERSTANDING RISK AND REWARD

Let's break down the concepts of risk and reward in investing using simple, relatable terms. Think of the financial market as a vast ocean. Just as the sea has calm and stormy days, the market has ups and downs. Your goal as an investor is to navigate these waters to reach the treasure island of financial gains while avoiding the pitfalls that could sink your investment ship.

Risk, in the investing world, is like the stormy weather or unpredictable sea conditions that can make your journey treacherous. This highlights the risk that you might not recover the money you've invested, with the worst-case scenario being a total loss. All investments come with some risk, influenced by market volatility, economic downturns, and geopolitical tensions. According to Britannica Money, financial markets can be vulnerable, with any sign of fear leading to uncertainty among investors (Gopalakrishnan, n.d.).

On the flip side, the reward is the sunny, calm day on the sea that makes your journey worthwhile. It tempts investors with the promise of potential gains, like finding treasure on your voyage. Investments that generally carry higher risks offer the potential for higher rewards to entice investors to take on those risks. Historically, stocks have outperformed bonds, offering higher returns due to their greater risk and potential for reward.

When considering an investment, it's crucial to balance these two elements. Imagine you're deciding whether to sail into open waters (investing in stocks) or stay close to the shore (keeping your money in a savings account). Staying close to the shore is safer, but you won't find much treasure. Venturing into open waters could lead to more outstanding discoveries (higher returns) and pose more risks.

Using real-life scenarios can further clarify this idea. For instance, if you're saving for a desired item, like a new smartphone or a vacation with friends, storing your savings under your mattress keeps it safe but stagnant. It won't increase in value. However, if you invest it, there's a chance it could grow faster, helping you reach your goal sooner. Yet, there's also the risk that you might end up with less than you started if the investment doesn't perform well.

Mastering the market's unpredictability demands grasping the risk-reward relationship, which acts as a navigational tool for investors through the financial terrain's complexities. Armed with this knowledge, you can now make choices that align with your financial goals and tolerance for risk, weighing the potential for gains against the possibility of losses.

The journey of investing is all about finding the right balance between risk and reward. By doing so, you aim to maximize your chances of reaching your financial goals while minimizing the chances of encountering a storm that could set you off course. Always remember that investing is a personal journey that requires careful consideration of your financial situation and goals.

Types of Financial Risks and Potential Rewards

Navigating the world of finance involves understanding various risks and seizing opportunities for rewards, especially for teens stepping into this arena. Let's dive into the different types of financial risks and how you, as a teenager, can manage these risks while aiming for potential rewards.

- **Market risk** involves the fluctuation of prices in financial instruments. Think of it as the risk of losing money in your investments due to changes in market conditions, like when stock prices fall. To tackle this, you could learn about the stock market's ups and downs and how to invest wisely, maybe starting with a simulation game or a small investment under a guardian's guidance.
- **Credit risk** occurs when someone fails to fulfill their financial obligations. Imagine you lend money to a friend, but they relocate and fail to repay the debt. Understanding the significance of maintaining good credit and managing debts is essential to reduce financial risk.
- **Liquidity risk** is about being unable to sell an asset without incurring a significant loss. For example, you face

liquidity risk if you buy sneakers as an investment but can't find buyers. Diversifying your investments across multiple asset classes helps mitigate the risk of concentrating all your funds on just one type of asset.

- **Operational risk** emerges from failures in business operations, such as poor management practices. This could mean a business you've invested in suffers losses because of ineffective management. Understanding how businesses run and the risks involved can guide you to make better-informed investment decisions.
- **Legal risk** involves financial loss due to legal proceedings. For teens, this could relate to understanding the legal aspects of any contracts or agreements you enter, like a phone or job agreement.

Turning risks into rewards involves seeking higher returns by effectively understanding and managing these risks. For instance, investing in stocks or starting a small business can offer significant rewards but come with risks that you need to understand and control.

Being intelligent in embracing financial risks can lead to innovation, growth, and economic stimulation by encouraging investment and job creation. Diversifying your investment portfolio is a practical way to manage risks, allowing you to explore various financial opportunities without putting all your eggs in one basket.

Grasping the balance between risks and rewards is essential for making choices that pave the way for financial success in the future. Engage with financial literacy programs, ask questions, and seek advice from trusted sources to build a solid foundation for your financial journey.

BALANCING RISK IN FINANCIAL DECISIONS

Navigating the world of finance, especially for teens, can seem like a daunting task. Yet, understanding how to assess and balance risk in various financial situations, such as investing or spending, is crucial for long-term success. Let's dive into some strategies that can help mitigate unnecessary risks and steer toward achieving your financial objectives.

Balance Risk by Diversifying Your Portfolio

Spreading your investments across different types of assets, such as stocks, bonds, and real estate, is essential for mitigating investment risk. This strategy is straightforward: if one investment dips, another might surge, balancing out potential losses. Imagine it as diversifying your portfolio instead of concentrating all your resources on a single option. This method minimizes risk because the failure of one investment doesn't necessarily doom the entire portfolio, acting as a financial safeguard for your assets.

Balance Risk by Investing in Long-Term Assets

Putting your money into long-term assets like stocks and real estate often proves to be a smart move. These types of investments typically offer higher returns over the long haul despite their tendency to fluctuate in the short term. Keeping a patient and long-term outlook can smooth out the emotional highs and lows of watching market changes.

Balance Risk Purposely Using Thoughtful Management Techniques

Thoughtful management involves regularly reviewing and adjusting your investment strategies based on market conditions and financial goals. It includes setting clear investment goals, understanding risk tolerance, and making informed decisions rather than reacting impulsively to market fluctuations.

Balance Risk by Recalibrating Your Portfolio

Your investment strategy should evolve in response to changes in your financial goals and market conditions. This evolution may involve adjusting your asset allocation to align your risk exposure with your preferences. For instance, if the value of your stock investments has increased significantly, making them a more significant part of your portfolio than you initially planned, you might consider selling some stocks and purchasing more bonds. This action helps in rebalancing your portfolio to its intended asset distribution.

Maximize Reaching Your Financial Objectives by Balancing Risk in Your Portfolio

Balancing risk in your investment portfolio is essential to increase the likelihood of achieving your financial goals. This means comprehending your objectives, time frame, and risk tolerance to construct a diversified portfolio that matches your goals. Consistently evaluating and adapting your investments when necessary can help you remain aligned with your objectives.

Have Multiple Sources of Income

Diversifying your income streams can also aid in mitigating financial risk. For example, if you run a laundromat, adding vending machines, arcade games, or offering a service to wash, dry, fold, and deliver clothes can provide additional sources of income, reducing the risk of financial downturns affecting your primary source of income.

Create a Risk Management Plan

A risk management plan includes how you will handle risks, encompassing your company's risk tolerance and the protocols for managing risk. This ensures everyone in the organization is on the same page and can help mitigate unnecessary risks.

Buy the Right Amount of Insurance

Insurance is essential for managing risk, but finding the right balance is crucial. You aim to avoid being inadequately insured and dealing with substantial out-of-pocket expenses for damages, nor do you want to overspend on premiums. Tailoring your insurance coverage to fit your needs can help manage this balance.

Hire a Risk Management Consultant

Consultants can offer expert advice on identifying, assessing, and managing risk, providing valuable insights that can help safeguard your financial future.

Keep Savings for Business Emergencies

Setting aside six to twelve months' worth of revenue can provide a financial cushion during difficult times, such as recessions or pandemics, ensuring your business remains operational.

Review Your Financial Risk Regularly

As your business grows and changes, the risks it encounters also evolve. Consistently assessing your risk management strategy guarantees its ongoing relevance and efficiency in safeguarding your financial assets.

By implementing these strategies, you'll adeptly navigate the financial terrain, making well-informed choices that weigh risks against rewards. This method safeguards your assets and lays the groundwork for economic prosperity and security.

LONG-TERM FINANCIAL PLANNING

Planning for your financial future might be different from your mind, especially when more immediate concerns and interests are vying for your attention. Starting early with financial planning can enhance your confidence, boost your savings and investment strategies, and improve your overall financial health. Here's why it's crucial, with advice tailored specifically for you as a teenager:

- **Boost your confidence with a written financial plan:** Having a financial plan isn't just for adults with complex assets; it's a tool that can help you, as a teenager, feel more confident about your money. A plan can guide your spending and saving, helping you make decisions that align with your goals, from saving for a concert ticket to planning for college expenses.
- **Kickstart your savings, no matter the amount:** It's a myth that you need a lot of money to start saving. Even small amounts, when saved consistently, can add up over time. Learning to save from an early age instills the habit of setting aside a portion of any money you receive from

part-time jobs, allowances, or gifts. This practice can help you build a savings cushion for future needs or desires.

- **Lay the groundwork for your investment portfolio:** While investing may feel distant, initiating it sooner allows you to maximize compound interest. You needn't wait until you amass a large sum. Beginning modestly with stocks or mutual funds enables gradual wealth accumulation. Remember, spending time in the market outweighs attempting to time it.
- **Cultivate better financial habits:** A financial plan can lead to the development of healthy financial habits. Mastering budgeting, saving, and maintaining a lifestyle aligned with your means are valuable skills that will benefit you throughout your lifetime. Learning to prioritize your spending on what truly matters to you, rather than succumbing to impulse buys or peer pressure, can significantly impact your financial future and personal happiness.
- **Tailor planning to your personality:** Financial planning isn't one-size-fits-all. Some strategies and tools can work for you whether you're a spender or saver, extroverted or introverted. Embracing your perspective on finances can enhance the enjoyment and effectiveness of financial planning. For example, if you're visual, you might use apps to track your savings goals, or if you're analytical, you might enjoy diving deeper into investment options.

Keep in mind that achieving financial independence is a personal and continuous journey. As you mature and your aspirations change, your financial strategy will evolve. The key is to begin, gain insights from your journey, and adjust accordingly. Your future self will appreciate your proactive approach.

HOW TO INCORPORATE RISK MANAGEMENT INTO LONG-TERM FINANCIAL PLANNING

Incorporating risk management into your long-term financial planning ensures you don't outlive your money and can gracefully handle economic and financial challenges. Effective risk management helps safeguard your savings and investment portfolios and avoid a scenario where limited financial options or increased debt become a reality during retirement. Let's break down how you can effectively integrate risk management strategies into your long-term financial plans, especially if you're a teenager starting to navigate these concepts.

First off, understanding the types of risks you might face is critical. These can range from market fluctuations and inflation to personal events such as job loss, illness, or unexpected expenses. Every type of risk requires specific strategies to reduce its effects. Risk management entails recognizing potential threats to your financial security, evaluating their consequences, and selecting and executing plans to manage them. It's crucial to continually assess the effectiveness of these plans to adjust to evolving situations.

For individuals, common risk management strategies include:

- **Risk avoidance:** Steering precise activities that could lead to financial harm. For instance, avoiding using credit for purchases to prevent debt-related risks.
- **Risk reduction:** To reduce potential losses, spread the risk by diversifying your investment portfolio.
- **Risk transfer:** Shifting the risk to another party, often through insurance policies, to protect against events like premature death, disability, or property damage.
- **Risk retention:** Accepting and managing the risk yourself might involve setting aside funds for potential

emergencies or opting not to insure certain manageable risks.

To integrate these strategies into your financial planning, establish precise financial objectives and gain insight into your risk tolerance. This helps in selecting the right mix of investments and insurance products. For example, if you're risk-averse, you might prioritize stable investments like bonds over volatile stocks or ensure comprehensive health and life insurance coverage.

Budgeting plays a crucial role as well. A solid budget helps manage your expenses and save for emergencies, reducing the need to rely on credit and lowering financial risk. Educating yourself on economic matters, such as the basics of investing, insurance, and the importance of an emergency fund, is also invaluable.

Remember, the goal of risk management in financial planning is not to eliminate all risk but to manage it in a way that aligns with your financial goals and risk tolerance. Interacting with a financial advisor or using resources from trusted financial education websites can offer customized guidance and strategies matching your circumstances.

For teens, approaching financial planning and risk management might seem daunting, but an early start gives you a significant advantage. By applying these strategies, you're protecting your current assets and securing your financial future.

REAL-LIFE EXAMPLES

Dive into the inspiring journeys of Tiffany Pham and Lauren Maillian, who turned financial challenges into entrepreneurial triumphs. Learn how Tiffany's coding nights and Lauren's early money smarts fueled their success. Their stories teach you the power of perseverance, savvy financial decisions, and unwavering work ethic.

Tiffany Pham

Tiffany Pham faced the towering challenge of student loans, yet her entrepreneurial spirit never wavered. With a vision for Mogul, a platform empowering working women, she didn't let financial obstacles deter her. Dedicating nights to teach herself coding while juggling day jobs, Tiffany's commitment was unwavering. She launched Mogul with a mere $200, a testament to her frugality and focus. Her journey is a beacon for teens, showing that financial hurdles can transform into stepping stones toward monumental success with hard work, ingenuity, and risk-taking. Tiffany's story is inspiring and a roadmap for overcoming financial risks and achieving dreams.

Lauren Maillian

Lauren Maillian started young, blending a childhood modeling career with savvy money management before turning twenty. At 19, she founded a winery, leveraging her early financial literacy into entrepreneurial success. Eschewing student loans, she chose state university, reflecting her acute understanding of financial risk and reward. Launching several companies and becoming the first Black woman to start a venture capital fund, Maillian's journey underscores her advice for young entrepreneurs: outwork everyone. Rejecting the notion of work-life balance, she champions work-life integration, embodying the ethos of investing time and energy now for future returns, always driven by an unmatched work ethic.

What You Can Learn From Tiffany Pham and Lauren Maillian

Tiffany Pham and Lauren Maillian offer powerful lessons on overcoming financial challenges and seizing success. Tiffany's journey with Mogul, starting from a place of financial constraint due to student loans, teaches teens the value of perseverance, self-education, and making the most of limited resources. By night, she armed herself with coding skills, and by day, she hustled at her job to launch her dream with just $200. Her story underscores that with determination and a clear vision, even the most daunting financial obstacles can become opportunities for growth and innovation.

Lauren Maillian's story, on the other hand, showcases the importance of early financial literacy and strategic risk-taking. Starting as a young entrepreneur and model, she carefully managed her earnings, which laid the foundation for her to dive into the wine industry at 19. By choosing education paths wisely and avoiding the trap of student loans, Lauren exemplifies how understanding financial risks and rewards from a young age is crucial. Her relentless work ethic and approach to work-life integration, rather than balance, highlight the importance of investing time and resources wisely for future gains.

Tiffany and Lauren embody the spirit of entrepreneurship, showing that age is just a number for financial savvy and business acumen. Their stories are invaluable lessons for teens: hard work, economic intelligence, and ingenuity can pave the way to achieving your dreams, no matter the financial hurdles you may face.

RISK VS. REWARD GAME

Imagine you're on a financial adventure, facing decisions that could shape your future wealth at each turn. Let's dive into some hypothetical situations to evaluate each option's risks and potential rewards. Remember, there's no right or wrong answer, just different paths to explore.

Scenario 1: Investing in Stocks

You've saved up $1,000 from your part-time job. Do you

- invest in a well-known, stable company's stock.
- take a chance on a small, volatile tech startup.

Risk vs. Reward

- Option A might offer steady but potentially lower returns. It's like choosing a safe path through the woods, where the journey is smooth, but the views are familiar.
- Option B could lead to significant gains if the startup succeeds, but you risk losing your investment. It's similar to trekking an unknown path with the chance of discovering a hidden waterfall or ending up lost.

Scenario 2: Starting a Business

You've got a great idea for a new app. Do you

- bootstrap the project, keeping your day job for financial stability.
- dive full-time into the startup, seeking investors for funding.

Risk vs. Reward

- Option A allows you to minimize financial risk by maintaining a steady income, but progress on your app may be slower. It's like building a raft piece by piece to ensure it floats.
- Option B is riskier, as you're putting all your eggs in one basket, but with potential investors, you could accelerate development and increase profits. It's like jumping into the river, hoping the current takes you to exciting new places faster.

Scenario 3: Saving for the Future

You want to start saving money. Do you

- put your savings into a traditional bank account.
- invest in a diversified mutual fund.

Risk vs. Reward

- Option A offers security and easy access to your money, but with low interest, the growth is minimal. It's akin to keeping your treasure buried in your backyard.
- Option B entails exposing yourself to market risks, yet it offers the possibility of achieving greater returns in the long run. It's similar to sending your ship to sea, where it could face storms and uncover new riches-filled lands.

As you encounter these situations, consider your individual goals, how much risk you're comfortable with, and the timeline for achieving your financial aims. Every decision you make on this journey shapes the path ahead, leading to new adventures and learning experiences. What path will you choose?

KEY TAKEAWAYS

- Risk and reward in investing are like navigating calm and stormy seas in pursuit of financial gains, with risks representing potential losses and rewards offering the promise of gains.
- Market volatility, economic conditions, and global events all play a role in determining the level of risk associated with every investment.
- Diversification, investing in long-term assets, and regular portfolio adjustments are vital strategies for balancing risk and aiming for financial success.
- Incorporating risk management into long-term financial planning involves understanding and mitigating risks through risk avoidance, reduction, transfer, and retention strategies.
- Setting clear financial goals, budgeting, and educating oneself on financial basics are essential to managing risk and securing an economic future.
- Starting early with financial planning and risk management can give teenagers a significant advantage in achieving long-term financial security and success.

Now's the time to leap! Use the lessons from Tiffany and Lauren's stories to tackle your financial challenges head-on. As we close this chapter on intelligent money management, gear up for the next adventure: mastering financial independence. Expect to dive deeper into taking control of your financial destiny, where every risk you take today crafts your tomorrow. Prepare yourself to transform your dreams into tangible realities!

A LIFETIME OF SUCCESS

As an author, I am excited to think that many of the skills you picked up in this book will help put you in the driver's seat of your financial future. Within these pages, you have found many true-life stories of teens just like you who made a mint from investing, starting a business, and diversifying their portfolio. With so many digital tools at hand and the knowledge contained in this book, I hope you are a much more empowered teen than you were before you discovered these simple yet proven steps to success.

IN UNDER 1 MINUTE
YOU CAN HELP OTHERS JUST LIKE YOU BY LEAVING A REVIEW!

Thank you so much for your support. I wish you a happy, fruitful life; may you always have the peace of mind that comes with financial stability.

Scan the QR code below

CONCLUSION

You learned practical financial management skills, such as budgeting, saving, and investing, through step-by-step guides, real-world examples, and interactive exercises tailored for teenagers. These methods made it easy to grasp and apply the concepts to your financial situation. Digital finance navigation became a breeze as you learned to use online banking and invest-ment apps wisely, empowering you to navigate the modern economic landscape confidently.

Building healthy financial habits became second nature to you. You developed responsible spending habits, made regular saving a priority, and learned to invest thoughtfully, setting yourself up for financial success in the long run. Understanding credit and debt management was no longer a mystery. You became familiar with credit scores, learned how to use credit cards responsibly, and understood the impact of debt, enabling you to make informed decisions in these areas.

Entrepreneurial thinking became a part of your mindset as you explored various ways to earn money. The book encouraged you to be self-reliant and innovative, fostering a sense of empowerment and independence. Compared to other financial guides that might have felt too broad or complex, this book spoke directly to you, using language and examples that resonated with your experiences and interests.

It provided a comprehensive yet simple overview of personal finance topics, breaking them into digestible segments for teenagers like you. The interactive elements, such as quizzes, worksheets, and real-life scenarios, made learning about finance engaging and practical. You found yourself more engaged and motivated to learn than traditional, more theoretical financial guides.

The book also addresses modern financial challenges unique to today's digital world, giving you a deeper understanding of the economic landscape you're growing up in. As a result, you gain confidence in making informed financial decisions, from everyday spending to long-term investments. You felt better prepared for adult financial responsibilities, reducing anxiety about future challenges like college expenses or independent living.

The skills and knowledge you've gained are the building blocks for achieving financial independence and security. You felt empowered to take control of your financial future, knowing you had the tools and expertise to reach your goals. Your enhanced financial awareness led to more responsible and thoughtful financial behavior, setting you up for success in the years to come. The book motivates you to take charge of your finances and build a stable financial future.

Keep expanding your financial knowledge. Stay curious, ask questions, and keep learning. The finance landscape is constantly changing, and you must change. Every wise financial decision you make today lays the groundwork for your future.

GLOSSARY

Asset allocation: This entails spreading investments among different asset classes, such as cash equivalents, bonds, and stocks.

Assets: Valuable possessions that you own and can convert into cash, such as savings accounts, investments, real estate, and personal property like electronics or bicycles.

Bonds: Investors in fixed-income securities lend money to entities like governments or corporations for a set period, receiving interest payments regularly and recouping their initial investment once the investment matures.

Budget: This plan helps you manage your money by monitoring your income and expenses, ensuring you live within your means, and setting aside savings for your financial goals.

Business plan: A document laying out the vision, objectives, strategies, and financial projections of a business venture, acting as a guide for achieving success.

Certificates of Deposit (CDs): Banks offer timed deposits where you agree to keep your money locked in for a set duration in return for a fixed interest rate.

Compound interest: Interest accumulates on the initial investment and the interest your investment has already earned.

Credit: Consider credit as a trust exercise involving money, wherein you currently borrow funds with a commitment to reimburse them in the future.

Credit report: A credit report is a detailed credit history record, including borrowing and repayment activities. Lenders use it to assess your creditworthiness.

Credit risk: Financial loss arises when an individual fails to meet financial obligations, such as repaying a loan.

Credit score: Your credit score serves as a report card on your financial habits, condensing your proficiency in handling borrowed funds into a three-digit number.

Custodial account: An account held in a custodian's name on behalf of a minor, often managed by a parent or guardian until the minor reaches legal adulthood.

Debt consolidation: This process involves consolidating several debts into one loan, which offers either a lower interest rate or repayment terms that are easier to manage.

Debt snowball method: A debt repayment strategy where you start by paying off your smallest debts first, gaining momentum and motivation as you see progress, and then moving on to more significant debts.

Digital finance: Using digital tools and technologies to manage personal and business finances, including online banking, budgeting apps, and digital payment systems.

Diversification: This involves spreading investments across different assets to reduce overall risk.

Emergency fund: This refers to funds allocated to handle unforeseen costs or financial crises, offering a buffer for economic security.

Estate planning: Organize the management and allocation of your investments and wealth after your death to guarantee the sufficient performance of your wishes.

Exchange-Traded Funds (ETFs): ETFs, similar to mutual funds, trade on stock exchanges and hold assets like commodities, bonds, and stocks.

Expenses: Money you spend on things like food, clothing, and entertainment.

50/30/20 Rule: This is a budgeting guideline where you allocate 50% of your funds for necessities, 30% for desires, and 20% for savings.

Financial goals: Goals you aim to achieve with your money include saving for college or purchasing a car.

Financial literacy: Understanding basic economic concepts and managing your money wisely.

Financial planning: This involves establishing financial objectives, devising strategies to attain them, and efficiently managing finances to ensure a secure financial future.

Financial tracking software: These apps or tools facilitate monitoring spending and saving habits, making it easier to manage your money and stay on top of your financial health.

High-yield savings accounts: Bank accounts that deliver higher interest rates than conventional savings accounts provide better returns on the money you deposit.

Income: Money you earn from sources like allowances, part-time jobs, or gifts.

Interest earnings: The additional money earned on top of the principal amount, typically expressed as a percentage.

Interest rates: This refers to the expense incurred when obtaining a loan. Typically presented as a percentage of the borrowed sum, it gets added to your overall debt.

IRA (Individual Retirement Account): A retirement savings account with tax advantages, allowing individuals to save for retirement with contributions invested in stocks, bonds, or mutual funds.

Insurance: A contract offering financial safeguarding against risks like damage or loss.

Investment: This involves allotting money with the anticipation of yielding profit or income.

Legal risk: Legal proceedings or contract disputes pose a risk of financial loss.

Liabilities: Your obligations to others, including debts or money you owe, like car loans, credit card debt, student loans, or mortgages.

Liquidity risk: This risk involves being unable to sell an asset without experiencing a substantial loss.

Market risk: Market conditions changing, such as a decline in stock prices, pose a risk of losing money in investments.

Money management: Effectively manage finances by budgeting, saving, investing, and controlling debt to attain financial goals and stability.

Mutual funds: Professional fund managers manage these investment vehicles, which pool money from numerous investors to purchase a diversified portfolio of securities such as bonds and stocks.

Net worth: This represents the variance between what you possess (assets) and what you must pay (liabilities). It is your economic scoreboard, indicating how effectively you manage your finances.

Operational risk: This risk results from poor management practices.

Portfolio: An individual or organization owns this collection of financial investments.

Principal: The investor or saver initially invests or saves a certain amount of money.

Retirement account (e.g., Roth IRA): An investment account designed to help you save and invest for retirement, offering tax advantages and compound growth potential over time.

Retirement planning: Develop a strategy to build up investment and savings to support your lifestyle post-retirement.

Risk management: Identifying potential threats to financial stability and implementing strategies to mitigate or address them, ensuring the long-term sustainability of savings and investments.

Risk tolerance: An individual's willingness to tolerate variability in investment returns.

Saving: Setting aside money for future use is a savvy decision that enables you to achieve your financial objectives, whether purchasing something you desire or planning for unforeseen expenses.

SMART goals: Specific, Measurable, Achievable, Relevant, and Time-bound goals designed to help you maintain control over your finances and achieve your objectives effectively.

Spending plan: Similar to a budget, a spending plan helps you allocate your money to different categories, ensuring you cover your needs and wants without overspending.

Stocks: These represent ownership shares in a corporation, asserting a share of a part of the company's acquisitions and profits.

Tax planning: Optimize your tax liabilities and maximize your after-tax income and savings using strategic tax planning techniques.

Tax return: A form you file with the government to report your income and calculate how much tax you owe or expect to receive as a refund.

Zero-based budgeting: Allocating every dollar you earn to specific expenses, leaving no money unassigned.

REFERENCES

Allcot, D. (2023, March 15). *Teens & taxes: Does your teen need to file taxes for their part-time job?* Yahoo Finance. https://finance.yahoo.com/news/teens-taxes-does-teen-file-184739773.html

Anglin, J. (2023, September 12). *Teens and taxes guide.* Kids' Money. https://www.kidsmoney.org/teens/taxes/

Aydin, R. (2020, August 6). *Erik Finman became a bitcoin millionaire at 18- now he's thinking about life beyond crypto.* The Business of Business. https://www.businessofbusiness.com/articles/erik-finman-bitcoin-millionaire-interview/

Budgeting for Teens: 14 tips for growing your money young. (2021, March 29). Mint. https://mint.intuit.com/blog/budgeting/budgeting-for-teens/

C., A. (n.d.). *22 goal setting statistics you should know in 2024 (Facts and studies).* HQ HIRE. https://hqhire.com/goal-setting-statistics/

Carosa, C. (2021, May 22). *True stories of children saving successfully.* Forbes. https://www.forbes.com/sites/chriscarosa/2021/05/22/true-stories-of-children-saving-successfully/?sh=5180fc5c2854

Deposit insurance at a glance. (2022, September 13). FDIC. https://www.fdic.gov/resources/deposit-insurance/brochures/deposits-at-a-glance/

Digital payments - Worldwide. (n.d.). Statista. https://www.statista.com/outlook/dmo/fintech/digital-payments/worldwide

Durante, A. (2022, October 18). *2023 tax brackets and federal income tax rates.* Tax Foundation. https://taxfoundation.org/data/all/federal/2023-tax-brackets/

Emergency funds explained for teens. (2022, July 4). Mydoh. https://www.mydoh.ca/learn/money-101/building-credit/emergency-funds-explained-for-teens/

Ferré, I. (2021, September 19). *Youth involved in the stock market 'is here to stay': Teen investor.* Yahoo Finance. https://finance.yahoo.com/news/youth-involved-in-the-stock-market-is-here-to-stay-teenage-investor-161706893.html

Fidelity study reveals teens think investing is important, but fewer than 1 in 4 have actually started. (2023, September 6). Fidelity Newsroom. https://newsroom.fidelity.com/pressreleases/fidelity--study-reveals-teens-think-investing-is-important--but-fewer-than-1-in-4-have-actually-star/s/fbe0e56c-bbf0-48d5-aa99-f9ce6282dae3

Forbes 30 under 30: Sanil Chawla. (n.d.). USC Iovine and Young Academy. https://iovine-young.usc.edu/the-pulse/forbes-30-under-30-sanil-chawla

Forgeard, V. (2023, August 9). *The power of persistence: Unraveling the importance of perseverance.*   Brilliantio.   https://brilliantio.com/why-is-perseverance-so-important/

Forrest, S. (2018, August 24). *Many young adults lack financial literacy, economic stability, study finds.* ScienceDaily. https://www.sciencedaily.com/releases/2018/08/180824135007.htm

Free 2024 budget planner and worksheets for a great year. (2023, November 16). Printables and Inspirations. https://www.printablesandinspirations.com/budget-planner-worksheets-printable/

Gensheimer, J. (2005, June 1). *More teens dealing with debt.* ParentMap. https://www.parentmap.com/article/more-teens-dealing-with-debt

Go Henry. "40 Quotes to Help You Learn the Value of Money." December 19, 2022. https://www.gohenry.com/us/blog/financial-education/40-quotes-to-help-your-child-learn-the-value-of-money

Gopalakrishnan, J. (n.d.). *Risk vs. reward in investing.* Britannica. https://www.britannica.com/money/risk-vs-reward

Grossman, A. L. (2023, February 16). *7 free teen budget worksheets & tools (Start your teenager budgeting).* Money Prodigy. https://www.moneyprodigy.com/teen-budget-worksheets/

Harley, L. (2022, April 6). *Survey: New research shows majority of teens feel unprepared to finance their futures.* Junior Achievement of Greater Washington. https://www.myja.org/news/latest/survey-new-research-shows-majority-of-teens-feel-unprepared-to-finance-their-futures

How much does the average teenager make? (2024). (2023, December 28). Kids' Money. https://www.kidsmoney.org/teens/earning/statistics/

How to rock your first credit card [Checklist]. (n.d.). Central Bank. https://www.centralbank.net/learning-center/how-to-rock-your-first-credit-card/

Kazdin, A. E. (2018, June 13). *Developing persistence, effort, and goal directed behavior in children and adolescents.* Alan Kazdin. https://alankazdin.com/developing-persistence/

Kosoff, M. (2023, August 28). *Do minors have to file taxes?* Keeper Tax. https://www.keepertax.com/posts/taxes-for-minors

Meet 16 teen founders who are building big businesses -- and making big money. (2019, August 20). Entrepreneur. https://www.entrepreneur.com/leadership/meet-16-teen-founders-who-are-building-big-businesses/337852

Michael. (2022, January 28). *Budget templates for teenagers.* Printable Formats. https://www.printableformats.com/budget-templates-for-teenagers/

Miller, K. (2022, October 2). *I'm only 15, but I have a plan to reach financial independence.* Business Insider. https://www.businessinsider.com/personal-finance/teenager-plan-reach-financial-independence-2022-9

Money management and budgeting tips for teens. (n.d.). Better Money Habits. https://

bettermoneyhabits.bankofamerica.com/en/personal-banking/money-manage ment-for-teens

Nair, D. (2021, August 16). *How teenage traders are turning their pocket money into profits.* The National. https://www.thenationalnews.com/business/money/ 2021/08/17/how-teenage-traders-are-turning-their-pocket-money-into-profits/

New research shows majority of teens feel unprepared to finance their futures. (2022, April 5). Business Wire. https://www.businesswire.com/news/home/ 20220405005734/en/New-Research-Shows-Majority-of-Teens-Feel-Unprepared-to-Finance-Their-Futures

Nickelsburg, M. (2016, September 16). *Young entrepreneurs share advice and success stories at Millennial Weekend Seattle.* GeekWire. https://www.geekwire.com/ 2016/young-entrepreneurs-share-advice-success-stories-millennial-weekend-seattle/

Plaut, A. (2023, July 10). *How to use a credit card wisely.* Benzinga. https://www. benzinga.com/money/how-to-use-a-credit-card-wisely

Radic, D. (2023, February 28). *Astonishing financial literacy statistics for 2024.* Moneyzine. https://moneyzine.com/personal-finance-resources/financial-literacy-statistics/

Riopel, L. (2019, June 14). *The importance, benefits, and value of goal setting.* Positive-Psychology.com. https://positivepsychology.com/benefits-goal-setting/

Sabatier, G. (2023, February 8). *18 ways teens can prepare for financial independence.* Millennial Money. https://millennialmoney.com/teens-financial-independence/

7 Important Saving Habits for Teens. (2023, April 28). Connections Academy. https:// www.connectionsacademy.com/support/resources/article/7-important-saving-habits-for-teens/

Sharpe, C. (2023, September 12). *23 best money apps for teens.* Kids' Money. https:// www.kidsmoney.org/teens/money-management/apps/

Sharpe, C. (2023, December 28). *How much money do teens have saved?* Kids' Money. https://www.kidsmoney.org/teens/saving/statistics

Simonetti, I. (2023, January 20). *How young people are saving money in a challenging economy.* The New York Times. https://www.nytimes.com/2023/01/20/busi ness/saving-money-inflation-economy.html

Survey finds 93% of teens believe financial knowledge and skills are needed to achieve their life goals. (2022, April 4). Business Wire. https://www.businesswire.com/news/ home/20220404005339/en/Survey-Finds-93-of-Teens-Believe-Financial-Knowledge-and-Skills-Are-Needed-to-Achieve-Their-Life-Goals

Tax filing requirements for children. (2023, December 11). TurboTax. https://turbo tax.intuit.com/tax-tips/family/tax-filing-requirements-for-children/L8ice6z0K

Teenage money management statistics hub. (n.d.). Money Prodigy. https://www.moneyprodigy.com/teenage-money-management-statistics/

Teen saving statistics [2023 study]. (n.d.). Kids' Money. https://www.kidsmoney.org/teens/saving/statistics/

Triffin, M. (2019, December 3). *How their emergency savings saved them.* Her Money. https://hermoney.com/save/emergency-fund/how-their-emergency-savings-saved-them/

Weissmann, J. (2012, March 12). *The misunderstood consequences of the student debt crisis.* Yahoo News. https://news.yahoo.com/news/misunderstood-consequences-student-debt-crisis-204030034.html

Young people's well-being: 2017. (2017, April 13). Office for National Statistics. https://www.ons.gov.uk/peoplepopulationandcommunity/wellbeing/articles/youngpeopleswellbeingandpersonalfinance/2017

Printed in Great Britain
by Amazon

42456764R00096